TRANSITION TO RETIREMENT AND ACTIVE AGEING:
Changes in Post-Retirement Lifestyles in Japan

Nobuhiko Maeda

University Education Press
Okayama, Japan 2008

Copyright © Nobuhiko Maeda 2008
First Published 2008
No part of this book may be reproduced in any form or by any means, print, photocopy, microfilm, or otherwise, without the prior written permission of the publisher.

CONTENTS

Acknowledgements v

Preface 1

Chapter 1 Introduction 5
    1. Approach to active ageing 5
    2. Social theory of ageing 7
    3. The paradigm of active ageing 10
    4. Active ageing studies in japan 11
    5. Active ageing vs. Productive ageing 15
    6. Analysis framework 18

Chapter 2 Retirees' Views on Work: Changes in Post-Retirement Lifestyles and Active Ageing 22
    1. Introduction 22
    2. Recent research directions 24
    3. Significance of mandatory retirement and occupational career 28
        3.1 Current status of post-retirement career development 28
        3.2 Assessing the significance of mandatory retirement 30
    4. Intentions regarding post-retirement career development and occupational autonomy 34
        4.1 Intentions regarding post-retirement career development 34
        4.2 Occupational autonomy and intentions regarding post-retirement career development 36
    5. Conclusions and discussion 41

Chapter 3 Transition to Later Life and Life Planning 47
    1. Transition to later life 47
    2. Life planning and willingness to work 48
    3. Contributing factors to willingness to work 51
        3.1 Assets/mortgage and willingness to work 51
        3.2 Life course and willingness to work 53
        3.3 Intention to become self-employed/start a business and willingness to work 55

    4. Logit analysis of willingness to work in later life *61*
    5. Summary and discussion *64*

Chapter 4   Transition to later life and quality of life *68*
    1. Introduction *68*
    2. Theoretical background. *69*
        2.1 Mandatory retirement, gender, and community resources   *69*
        2.2 Mandatory retirement, bridge jobs, and work-life habits   *71*
    3. Methods. *72*
        3.1 Data and analysis   *72*
        3.2 Analysis and manipulated variables   *73*
    4. Results *75*
        4.1 Mandatory retirement and occupational careers   *75*
        4.2 Gender differences in the process of mandatory retirement   *78*
        4.3 Men's occupational attitude and life adjustments   *80*
    5. Conclusions and discussion *81*

Chapter 5   Social Networks in Later Life. *88*
    1. Social isolation of the elderly *88*
    2. Concept of social networks *90*
    3. Studies on the social networks of Japanese elderly *93*
    4. Social network structure of the elderly *95*
    5. Typology of social network *100*
    6. Personal community building *105*

Chapter 6   Personal Community of Elderly in Urban Situation *110*
    1. Introduction *110*
    2. Concept of personal community *111*
    3. Cases. *113*
    4. Conclusions and discussion *119*

Chapter 7   Social Networks in Later Life and the Quality of Life. *123*
    1. Approach to the quality of life *123*
    2. Earlier studies *123*
        2.1 Quality of life and subjective well-being   *123*
        2.2 Social networks and subjective well-being   *124*

3. Results 126
      3.1 Distribution of morale   126
      3.2 Distribution of health conditions and morale   128
      3.3 Personal community and subjective well-being   130
   4. Personal community and the quality of life. 132

Chapter 8 Summary and Conclusion. 137
   1. Summary. 137
   2. General and policy implications. 141
      2.1. Active ageing and citizenship. 141
      2.2. Life course perspective and employment/labor policies 143
      2.3. Diversified lifestyles in a later life and lifelong learning policy . . . 145

Referrences 147

Acknowledgements

This is a partial English translation of "Sociology of Active Ageing: Elderly, Work and Social Network," published by Minerva Press in 2006.

Some chapters of this book are based on papers presented in scholarly journals, as shown below. The original papers were all written in Japanese.

Chapter 2   Retirees' Views on Work: Changes in Post-Retirement Lifestyles and Active Ageing. *Japanese Sociological Review*, Vol.56, No.1, pp.55-73 (2005).

Chapter 3   Middle-aged Workers' Life Plan after Retirement: The Way of Working Life and Life Plan of Middle-aged Generation in Japan. Japan Institute of Labour (JIL) Research paper series. No.118, pp.14-27 (1998).

Chapter 4   Retirement Transition and Its Impacts on the Quality of Life: A Study on the Gender Comparison of the Mandatory Retirement Process. *Ritsumeikan Sociological Review*, Vol.41, No.1, pp.111-131 (2005).

Chapter 5   Family and Social Network of the Elderly. *The Journal of the Institute of Household Economy*, Vol.40 (Autumn), pp.35-43 (1998).

Chapter 6   Personal Community of Elderly People in Urban Situation.
The Journal of the Tokyo Institute for Municipal Research, Vol.86, No.9, pp. 41-52 (1995).

Chapter 4 was also published in "Quality of Life in Japan and the Netherlands," Kit Niod Encounters Series, edited by Joop Stam and Ruud Veenhoven (2007).

I would like to take this opportunity to express my thanks to everyone who has been so much a part of the journey of this book, with special thanks to Minerva Press, from which my original work written in Japanese was published and which kindly gave me permission to undertake a partial translation of the book and its publication.

This English version of the book will come to the world under Ritsumeikan University's 2007 grants scheme for the publication of scholarly books. My gratitude continues to Ritsumeikan University and PALABRA, the word company, which cooperated in the translation of the book from Japanese to English.

I close with giving thanks to my wife, Shino, who support me, and my two sons, Satoshi and Hitoshi, both of whom always give me great energy and vitality. I believe that without my family support, it would be difficult for me to pursue my research activities on weekends and holidays, while devoting weekdays to teaching and related work.

Preface

This book sheds light on the important factors involved in leading an active, high-quality life at a later stage of life. Especially, focus is placed on the effects of post-retirement jobs and social networks on elderly people's lives.

I compiled papers that I worked on over the past decade into a book. In this book, therefore, some chapters overlap in substance and arguments. To ensure consistency as a book and improve its readability, I significantly revised and reorganized the contents of the papers on which this book is based.

The basic questions discussed in this book are as follows.

① *Can the notion of active ageing be seen in the later life planning of Japanese people? In other words, the question is about whether older people can play an active role in creating a welfare society in a broad sense — rather than passively spending their later life as a welfare client — by remaining in the labor market or involving themselves in the local community.*

② *How do Japanese older people adapt themselves to the retirement system? Can quality of life be improved through continued work? Is withdrawal from the workforce a necessary condition for better adaptation to mandatory retirement? Or is there any difference in adaptation to retirement between men and women?*

③ *What relations are there between social relationships — the notion of "social networks" used in this book — and the quality of life in later life? What kind of social networks are more effective in improving older people's quality of life?*

Following from the question outlined above, this book consists of eight chapters.

Chapter 1 gives an introduction to the concept of active ageing and provides the basic framework of this book.

Chapter 2 presents a diversified lifestyles and vocational career development in later life, by defining a life stage from middle life to later life, with retirement as a turning point. In this chapter I will reveal the fact that a new social norm for active ageing has come to appear among so-called baby-boomers and younger generations in Japan.

Chapter 3 identifies baby boomers' willingness to continue to work in the later stage of life through data analyses concerning transition from middle life to later life and life planning.

Chapter 4 conducts a gender comparative analysis of mandatory retirement and the quality of post-retirement life. Especially, focus is placed on women's involvement in the local community and the effects of men's employment in bridge jobs to quality of life.

Chapter 5 examines the situation of active social relationships in later life, from the perspective of social networks.

Chapter 6 takes a case study approach to social networks in later life. Social networks of older people and an urban community are discussed, with a notion of a personal community.

Chapter 7 analyzes the influence of a personal community on the quality of later life. In particular, it is proved that when personal communities are classified, the "liberated" type of social networks contributes most to improving the quality of elderly people's lives.

Chapter 8 provides a summary and conclusion. Policy implications on active ageing are also proposed here.

Introduction

Chapter 1

1. Approach to active ageing

In Japan, the first wave of baby-boomers (born in 1947 to 49) will reach retirement age in 2007. With the transition into a full-fledged aged society, the Japanese government needs to carry out radical reforms in its labor policies and social security system. In April 2006, a significant amendment was made to the Law concerning Stabilization of Employment of Older Persons, under which companies are required to take measures to provide employment security for older workers until the age of 65. The purpose of this law amendment is to promote the employment of older people. By 2013, employers will be obliged to endeavor to raise retirement age, introduce a continued employment system, abolish the employees' mandatory retirement system at the age of 60, or conduct other necessary measures in order to secure stable employment for older workers.

The ageing of the population is a problem confronting not only Japan but also Western countries and China, which still has its one-child per family policy. To revise/restructure the social system in preparation for the coming aged society is an issue we must face. In fact, European countries are pressing ahead with plans to reverse the trend of early exit from the labor market and encourage late exit. Thus, institutional measures to address the ageing population is going to be a common issue shared by Japan and other industrialized countries.

In terms of international policy developments, the International Labor Organization (ILO) has promoted the employment of older citizens, and the World Health Organization (WHO) has proposed the improvement of health in later life. In respect of promoting active ageing, they are on common ground. To reflect such international policies in Japan, it is necessary to grasp the current situation of working patterns and lifestyles of elderly people through empirical analyses by introducing notions that embody various factors, such as employment/work, lifestyle, social involvement and health.

This book aims to identify and analyze the status of older Japanese people's working patterns and attitude toward work, based on the concept of "active ageing," and to shed light on some aspects of the working life of older persons from a sociological perspective. With the keyword of "active ageing," this book underlines the concept that elderly people should actively participate in society and play a part in supporting society through their continued work and involvement in social activities, rather than as the target of welfare. However, this book focuses not only on employment but also on the "optionality" and "diversity" of life courses, which allow elderly people to have a choice to work or participate in volunteer and other social activities. In other words, this book places more importance on the idea that at a time when the labor force is shrinking because of the falling birthrate and the ageing population, a social system should be created in which more job opportunities are given to elderly people who are in good health and are willing to work, rather than the idea that all the elderly should be put into the labor market. Furthermore, the term "active ageing" referred to in this book is a comprehensive notion that includes invalided elderly as well as those who are physically in good condition. This is based on the idea that elderly people, even if they have mobility impairments, can decide about their lives for themselves.

One of important issues in analyzing the later stage of life from these perspectives is a diversity of life. Owing to its large population, the baby boomer generation tends to be viewed as a homogeneous cohort. However, data on the same cohort (same birth year group) show that they are very diverse in their life courses, lifestyles, ways of thinking and health levels. As the health level of those in the later stage of life is widely diverse, compared to when they were young, a primary objective in recent social gerontological studies is to identify the diversity of ageing and clarify what factors are attributable to it. In a policy debate concerning this issue, more emphasis has been placed on support for self-determination and self-reliance while respecting a diversity of lifestyles among elderly people. Taking into account policy support for diverse lifestyles in later life, this book explores the future direction of employment policy by shedding light on some aspects of various lifestyles in later life using recent data as a fundamental effort to create a social framework within which to provide diverse opportunities for active ageing.

2. Social theory of ageing

In the fields of sociology and social gerontology, what kinds of approaches have been taken toward ageing thus far? The approach to active ageing taken by this book aims to present a new paradigm for perceiving an aged society and is based on the accumulation of empirical and theoretical studies. The historical development of social theory of ageing is briefly reviewed as follows (Atchley and Barusch, 2004; Hooyman and Kiyak, 1995; Johnson et al., 2005; Victor, 2005).

Research on ageing has been promoted, centering on gerontology. Gerontology can be approached from three aspects: biological theory, psychological theory and sociological theory. In any theory, empirical research based on surveys and data analyses is important. At the same time, a theory construction to explain the results of analysis also plays a key role.

In gerontology, many findings have been obtained through empirical research, based on which theory construction has been carried forward. These days, however, many empirical studies presented in academic journals suggest that researchers and practitioners show less interest in theorizing about ageing (Johnson et al., 2005: 5). From the biological aspect of ageing, for example, many researchers tend to focus on empirical models for the description of ageing at the cell or molecular level, gradually departing from the trend of theoretical integration with other fields.

Ageing studies in sociology is no exception and has fallen behind in theory construction. While empirical studies have been accumulated, approaches for theoretically explaining significant social phenomena remain stagnant, such as the consequences of the ageing of the population, changes in personal status resulting from an ageing society, and mutual dependence between different age groups/generations (Johnson et al., 2005: 5).

The field of social gerontology, which is a sociological approach to ageing, is often characterized by the lack of theoretical development since more emphasis is placed on problem solving than theory, compared to biological and behavioral science approaches to ageing (Johnson et al., 2005:13). In addition to some traditional theories, however, new theory approaches are being taken up these days.

Under these circumstances, the American sociologist R. Atchley developed theories of ageing through research into retirement. In a social gerontology book co-edited with A. Barusch, Atchley divides the sociological approach to ageing into three aspects (Atchley and Barusch, 2004). The first is microsocial theories, which include the disengagement theory, stress and coping theory, and continuity theory, all of which focus on the ageing of individuals. The second is micro-macro theories, which center on how macro social changes have an impact on the ageing of individuals. One of its representative approaches is the life-course theory. The third aspect is macro social theories, which exist in large numbers in gerontology. Among them, representative theories are the modernization theory, societal disengagement theory, and structural lag theory. Atchley et al. argue that worthy of special note is that these theories are not exclusive to one another. In other words, most important is what theory is used to explain the process of the ageing of specific people, rather than which theory is right or wrong.

M. Johnson, V. Bengtson and other American gerontologists, who more comprehensively reviewed gerontological theories, have employed a more detailed classification of the sociological theories of ageing (Johnson et al., 2005). According to them, earlier theories concerning ageing were established by Linton (1942), Parsons (1942), and Havighurst (1954). These sociologists integrated their findings obtained through empirical studies into theoretical analysis to derive four first-generation theories in social gerontology: disengagement theory, activity theory, modernization theory, and subculture theory.

The second-generation theories in social gerontology were developed between 1970 and 1985, consisting of the continuity theory, social breakdown/competence theory, exchange theory, age stratification perspective, and in addition, political economy of ageing perspective. From the late 1980s onward, these theories were elaborated upon and reconstructed, and more theories were added.

Major social gerontological theories put forward from 2000 until now include a life course perspective, age stratification perspective, social exchange theory, social constructionist perspective, feminist theory of ageing, political economy of ageing perspective, critical perspective of ageing, and postmodernism.

Active ageing, which is the core concept of this book, is basically a direct extension of the above-mentioned social theories of ageing, and some researchers consider it to be derived from the activity theory in social gerontology (Mandin, 2004). One of the most striking characteristics of active ageing is that the concept came to attract attention as part of international ageing policy efforts mainly by the International Labor Organization (ILO) and the World Health Organization (WHO). In fact, Johnson et al. (2005) introduced active ageing in detail by creating a separate section of global ageing, in which the concept is regarded as a global-scale strategy that covers both advanced and developing countries (Johnson et al., 2005: 43). As described later, A. Walker from Britain and other sociologists, who have played a central role in ageing policies in the EU, are now working on the notion of active ageing more elaborately from a theoretical perspective (Walker, 2002; Mandin, 2004).

3. The paradigm of active ageing

How is active ageing viewed at the policy or research level?

The concept of active ageing has been actively employed in the development of international policies particularly since the latter half of the 1990s, and in recent sociological studies.

The ILO, which has already adopted recommendations concerning the improvement of older people's labor conditions (ILO Recommendation No. 162, 1980) at its general assembly, recently emphasized that the increase in the aged population is a common issue shared by advanced nations and that a system that allows people to have job opportunities in later life should be established. The organization has also proposed to take active policy measures to eliminate age discrimination in employment and enhance the employability of older people in particular (ILO, 2002; Taqi, 2002). The ILO has centered on the employment of older people, or their participation in the labor market, whereas the WHO's policy objective is to maintain health in later life by promoting the social involvement of older people and enhancing their quality of life. In this respect, the WHO is more comprehensive in policy strategies than the ILO. The WHO brought the concept of active ageing to the fore in a policy report published in 2002, having a great influence on research in the fields of health and medicine, social gerontology, and sociology (WHO, 2002; Walker, 2002).

The WHO (2002) defines the concept of "active ageing" as follows:

Active ageing is the process of optimizing opportunities for health, participation, and security in order to enhance quality of life as people age. (WHO, 2002: 12)

The term "active" referred to here not merely means participation in the labor market or a physically active condition. It also implies continued involvement in social, economic, cultural or mental activities and civil activities. In short, this is based on the premise that older people who have already retired from the workforce, who are in poor health or who have disabilities can be part of society as an active contributor to their families, friends, communities and the nation. Therefore, the WHO's policy ideas include the perception that the ultimate goal of active ageing is to improve quality of life by extending the healthy life expectancy of all the elderly, including those in need of care (WHO, 2002).

4. Active ageing studies in Japan

In line with active ageing policies actively promoted by the WHO and the ILO, empirical studies have been introduced in Japan as well to explore the potential of active ageing, by posing a question: What conditions are required to encourage active ageing in later life?

The domains of social medicine and public health have started to employ the concept of active ageing from the perspective of health maintenance in later life (Tsuji, 2004). For active ageing, importance is placed on the social participation of elderly people, and a new concept of "healthy life expectancy" has been put forward.

The field of social gerontology has also started to pay attention to the concept of active ageing (Koyano & Ando, 2003). The conventional idea of "productive ageing" has caused concern in that its emphasis on the elderly's participation in economic activities may force older people to work, as well as criticism regarding its making light of how mental/internal activities play an important role. In response, the slogan "Active Ageing" of the International Year of Older Persons (1999) was proposed as an issue to create a desirable lifestyle in later life, while valuing diversity in individuality and needs of older people. Empirical research in social gerontology in Japan has advanced centering on the themes of "successful ageing" and "quality of life," inspired by the idea of active ageing (Koyano & Ando, 2003; Naoi, 2001).

The perspective of active ageing has also come to the fore in the field of sociology. Mamoru Funatsu indicates the importance of changing the image of elderly people (Funatsu, 2003). He argues that in today's society where ageing has a strong negative image, the question in older people's minds now is how they can avoid ageing. In other words, a matter of great interest is for them to avoid such negative situations as becoming bedridden and senile. However, Funatsu claims that a new norm should be created for positively accepting the process of ageing, rather than brushing "ageing" under the carpet or rejecting age-induced deterioration of mental/physical functions. He proposes: "re-construction of older people's self-identity" (Funatsu, 2003: 49-54). He argues that the process of ageing is more a sense of loss, during which people enter into a period of maturity via changes/improvements, rather than deterioration. He adds that older people can reconstruct the past, based on which they can generate new meaning for the present, and that new meaning can be created by deriving meaning from the past and reinterpreting the present" (Funatsu, 2003: 53). He also emphasizes the importance of creating an active ageing culture, saying that even if older people receive care from others through active social participation, "it means to aim for the 'active ageing' that can create something new by changing themselves from a mere object to a subject through coexistence of dependence and independence," rather than excessive dependence (Funatsu, 2003: 52).

Isamu Kaneko, a Japanese urban sociologist, claims that it is necessary to get rid of the conventional positioning of older people as those in the "process of shrinking their roles" and to establish their image as those in the "process of maintaining, restoring or creating their roles." He proposes to redress a widely accepted conventional image of elderly people being a "dependent" (Kaneko, 1998). The Japanese urban sociologist Kiyoshi Morioka also made the same suggestion (Morioka, 2000). Morioka indicates in his research on older people's personal networks, that in today's society there is a significant change in the norm of elderly people who support a "retirement" culture. He argues that under the influence of the past family norm, the roles played by grandparents in a three-generation family contribute to a conventional image of older people. The practice of retiring from active life has demanded older people's withdrawal from the labor market and presents a desirable image of elderly people, based on the premise that they gradually transfer their headship of the family and change their roles from the representative of a family to those enjoying their retirement and spending the rest of life with their children and grandchildren. Japan's traditional image of older people has been presented concretely as mellow, retired people (Morioka, 2000: 163). Because of a widely accepted image of older people as those calmly spending their rest of life with their children and grandchildren, elderly people who are active and have a strong personality used to be regarded as a deviation from the conventional desirable image of older people. Recently, however, there has been an increase in the number of older people who break down such a conventional image. Morioka indicates that a gradual change has been seen in the image of older people from the conventional one of retiring from active life, to a more active one. He says, "The image of older people who actively enjoy an urban life and have a strong personality seems to have already been established" (Morioka, 2000: 164).

Based on the WHO's definition of active ageing, the sociologist Toshikatsu Oda characterized the concept using four factors: (1) Active ageing does not merely mean physically active. (2) It means a contribution to family, friends, local community and society through continued participation/involvement in social, economic, mental, cultural or political events. (3) Independence, participation, dignity, caring, and self-fulfillment are the rule. (4) The image of older people has changed from the status as a target of caring to an individual with rights (Oda, 2003).

In addition, Oda put forward the "third age" concept, which he argues is as important as active ageing (Oda, 2003). The "third age" is the idea that a course of life can be divided into four stages and the third stage (so-called the third age), which is longest, is regarded as a period for achievement/accomplishment/fulfillment (Oda, 2003: 10). It is generally defined as the stage from the age of about 40 or 50 to the period when people find it difficult to live an independent life (Oda, 2003: 11). The "first age" that starts at the moment of birth means a period of being dependent/immature/nurtured. The "second age" is a period of independence/work/child-raising/saving, and the "third age," a period of achievement/accomplishment/fulfillment. The "fourth age" is characterized as a period of dependence/senile deterioration/death.

Withdrawal from the labor market, including mandatory retirement, is merely point during the third age. What is important is to think about how to spend the third age as a whole, not about how to spend the rest of life by separating post-retirement life from pre-retirement life. In addition, an "active lifestyle" should be established during the third age. As Oda argues, the "third age" concept does not regard mandatory retirement as a turning point, and the stage refers to the period of second growth that follows the second age. This also suggests that people can continue to grow and develop even after middle age. (Oda, 2003)

5. Active ageing vs. Productive ageing

The British sociologist, social gerontologist Alan, Walker, who has been actively involved in EU ageing policies, is very stimulating in that he theoretically organized the concept of active ageing (Walker, 2002). According to Walker, "active ageing" is a concept developed in the 1990s under the influence of the WHO, and therefore it is closely related to "activity" and "health" in later life and puts a premium on "healthy ageing." The concept of active ageing came into use mainly in European nations, whereas the notion of "successful ageing" has been employed in the U.S. since as early as the 1960s. Active ageing is a concept of the activity theory that was put forward as an objection to the disengagement theory where it is inevitable that the roles played and social relationships developed until middle age are lost in later life (Cumming and Henry, 1961; Havighurst, 1954).

In the 1980s, "productive ageing" attracted attention as a new concept introduced in response to the development of social policies in the U.S. In those days, the concept was coined within the context that needs of researchers, older people and policymakers were matched. Some researchers embarked on life-course research and started to argue that chronological age cannot be considered a good variable to predict activity in later life. At the same time, a life-course approach came to be applied to ageing studies. Researchers started to expand their interests toward human development throughout a course of life, not by focusing only on the late stage of life. It can be said that the notion of productive ageing was theoretically borne out by the accumulation of ageing studies actively approached from the dynamic life-course perspective of lifelong human development and historical changes.

In fact, older people in the U.S. tend to pursue social activities after withdrawal from the labor market, rather than following a traditional lifestyle where they enjoy leisure time or take care of their families. In this respect, productive ageing is closely matched to the needs of older people who search for a more active lifestyle. At the same time, such movements to seek for more active later life were accepted by policymakers for whom pension and healthcare cost issues resulting from the ageing of the population and enhancement of labor productivity are a big concern. At the G8 summit held in Denver, the U.S. in 1997, the representatives of participating countries discussed to the possible removal of disincentives to entering the labor market and barriers that prevent part-time employment. In this context, the promotion of employment and social participation of older people were gradually linked to the concept of "productive ageing" (Walker, 2002).

Thus, the concept of "successful ageing" or "productive ageing," rather than "active ageing," has been actively employed in the U.S. However, Walker claims that since the "productive ageing" concept tends to focus on the production of goods and services, it is likened to being "instrumental" and "economistic" (Walker, 2002: 123). It is because being "productive" is associated with activities for producing goods and services that "have to be paid for."

In contrast, the concept of "active ageing" does not only place emphasis on production of goods and older people's participation in the labor market. It also focuses on various activities in a broader sense and attaches importance to the inclusion and participation of older people as citizens. This concept was developed as a general life-style strategy to maintain physical or mental health as long as possible, not based on the limited view of encourageing elderly people to work longer (Walker, 2002: 124). Active ageing is a broader concept that includes central elements of the "productive ageing" concept and that places particular emphasis on the quality of life and psychological/physical well being (European Commission, 1999).

From this perspective, Walker advocates seven principles concerning active ageing (Walker, 2002).

The first principle is that activity in later life should not be limited to paid employment or production activity and that it should consist of "all meaningful pursuits" that contribute to older people themselves, their families and local communities, and the well-being of society in a broader sense.

The second is that the concept of active ageing is targeted for every older person, including those in poor health and living as a dependent. This aims to prevent the risk of focusing only on "young-old" people and excluding the "old-old" people.

The third is that active ageing is a preventive concept. This means an actively ageing process in a course of life. In short, this concept is true of not only older people but also all age groups.

The fourth principle is that the active ageing concept gives importance to the maintenance of intergenerational solidarity. Fairness between generations is important to enable younger generations as well as older generations to lead an active future life.

The fifth is that active ageing is a concept that involves both "rights" and "obligations."

The sixth principle is that active ageing is about promoting social participation and empowerment of older people. In other words, top-down policies that allow and encourage elderly people to participate in various kinds of activities have to be combined with opportunities for bottom-up activities.

The last principle is that active ageing must respect the national and cultural diversity.

These seven principles of active ageing suggest that the concept is based on a partnership between "citizens" and "society." Under this partnership, the role played by the state is to promote or enable older people's activities based on their citizenship and, as need arises, to provide them with high-quality social protection as long as possible (Walker, 2002: 125). Thus, Walker reconstructed the concept of active ageing from a broad perspective ranging from the micro level of health to the macro level of social policies as implementation measures. In fact, the concept Walker reconstructed was used as the theoretical backbone of ageing policies in the EU. The above-mentioned observations are very suggestive in carrying empirical studies concerning ageing forward and offering policy prescriptions for ageing society in Japan.

Various studies on the recently developed concept of active ageing were introduced in this chapter. Despite minor differences among researchers in the definition of active ageing, as shown in individual studies, there is a consensus on the "process of ageing": people should live an active life in middle and later life while accepting the inevitable "deterioration" of their functions Therefore, it can be said that it implies the emergence of a new cultural/social norm to support creative ageing, which can replace the traditional retirement culture.

6. Analysis framework

This book empirically analyzes the present situation of elderly people in Japan, based on the above-mentioned concept of active ageing. In particular, the possibility of active ageing in Japan is discussed from three perspectives.

The first perspective is "active ageing". As mentioned earlier, it is based on the idea that older people are not merely socially vulnerable but can also play a role in supporting society (Walker, 2002). As in EU policies concerning the employment of older people, the idea also includes the promotion of social participation of all people, regardless of age (Hamaguchi, 1999, 2000, 2003). As a matter of course, the strength and health of people in later life is lower than in early life. Elderly people are also diverse in their health conditions and lifestyles. However, it is necessary to reevaluate the positioning of elderly people. All the elderly should not be protected as the vulnerable, but they could be more actively involved in society as important social contributors by taking full advantage of their abilities. To this end, elderly people's participation in society should not be limited to the labor force of companies. It should be regarded as social activities including volunteer and local-community-related activities. In short, it is important to view elderly people from the perspective that they create a social network, which goes beyond corporate activities and includes a wide variety of activities in non-profit organizations and local communities.

This "active ageing" concept overlaps with the view that those in later life are diverse in their lifestyles. Following the upcoming mass retirement of the baby-boomer generation, the arrival of the aged society is often talked about. Although they are in the same cohort, their lifestyles are very different. Some are willing to remain in the workforce after mandatory retirement, and some desire to enjoy the slow life on a pension. The aged society will invite more diverse lifestyles of older people. As shown in this book, there is no specific model of older people's work life since there are various working patterns for people aged over 60 depending on their assets, savings, willingness to work and working environment. The model of active ageing should be built on the premises that elderly people are diverse in their health and economic conditions. In this respect, each older person needs to look for the work pattern and lifestyle most suitable for them. Japanese men tend to live a life based on a company-oriented social network. In later life, however, organization men, who are immersed in their business careers, may develop a new social network, for example, by going into business for themselves or getting jobs through temporary staffing agencies.

For elderly people, the reality of employment is not regarded so optimistically. However, there is an option to work part-time while drawing a pension. Or some people may remain full-time workers after mandatory retirement by renewing a contract with the company they are currently working for. In contrast, not a few people are expected to actively devote themselves to volunteer activities after retirement. Thus, the working patterns and lifestyles of the elderly will become more diversified. What is selected from among a diversity of life planning patterns is left to the judgment of the individual. From a sociological perspective, it can be said that the scope of options of lifestyles available to elderly people will be increasingly widened and that individualism will be fostered. This book views the diversity of elderly people's working patterns and lifestyles as an important notion.

The second perspective is "life-course" (Elder, 1974). Ageing policies should be discussed from the perspective that a lifestyle in later life is a result of lifestyle habits in early life. In fact, a post-retirement lifestyle is significantly affected by what career is pursued and what work-life pattern is established from early life. In later-life occupational career studies, therefore, consideration should be given to the accumulation of careers and the development of lifestyle habits from early to middle life. Some European countries have made efforts to reverse the early retirement trend and, in response to the prolonged working life, began to develop policies to redistribute working time over the life course. European governments have made a shift in their policies from conventional work-life patterns, in which people have long working time in the prime of life and considerably reduce their working hours in later life, to more flexible work-life patterns. These polices emphasize the balance between personal and work life, taking account of personal working-time preference. In a word, European countries are on track to increase the flexibility of the entire working life by allowing people to design a later-life occupational career when they are in early and middle life. Thus, ageing cannot be defined just as later life or a stage of life course, but it begins from career design in early life. This book considers the life-course perspective to be very important in approaching active ageing.

The third perspective is "social network". In the later stage of life, the weight of jobs in life decreases, and the importance of relations with the local community and family increases. Given this, more discussions should be made on active ageing in later life not only from the perspective of occupational careers, but also with more focus on a diversity of social networks, including relations with family, neighborhood/local community and friends. In this book, approaches are made in regard to relations with various people in later life from the perspective of "social networks." Social network theory, which is a field of sociology developed in the region of family sociology or urban sociology, has brought many empirical studies on the social relations of people other than the elderly. The concept of social networks is useful in analyzing social relations that cannot be effectively construed with conventional structural concepts such as "groups."

Grounded on those social network studies, this book is concerned with active ageing. In addition, concepts and framework by B. Wellman, a Canadian urban sociologist, is applied to analyses of older people in Japan (Wellman, 1981; Hall and Wellman, 1985). Worthy of special note is the use of the "personal community" concept that refers to the relations of people beyond the scope of neighborhoods. The term "community" tends to be associated with the "local community" confined to a specific area, but the personal community concept used in this book differs from conventional community concepts. This book actively applies the "social network" theory and "personal community" to bring out new practical implications for community policies in ageing society.

In sum, the main issues discussed in this book can be represented by the three keywords: "active ageing," a "diversity of occupational career opportunities," and a "social network." Based on these keywords, this book empirically analyzes various aspects of active ageing. This book also aims to present comprehensive policy implications to accommodate shifts in paradigm in preparation for the upcoming aged society.

Retirees' Views on Work: Changes in Post-Retirement Lifestyles and Active Ageing

Chapter **2**

1. Introduction

In the context of longevity extension and falling birthrate, Japan's population is ageing at an alarming rate, and the arrival of a super-ageing society is expected in the 21st century. The advancement of the ageing society is also having a tremendous impact on the current employment system. Especially, in the 1990s, when the bubble economy burst and the country experienced a prolonged economic slowdown, significant changes were observed mainly in the environment surrounding middle-aged and older employees. These include restructuring of the seniority system, the encouragement of early retirement, and transfer to subsidiaries (Inagami 1999, Sato 1999). At the same time, the graying of the country is having a considerable influence on the age structure charts of companies. Since the 1980s, the percentage of those aged 55 or above to the total number of employees are steadily on the increase. In terms of work force, an increasing number of small-size enterprises have found it difficult to do without workers of advanced years (Japan Organization for Employment of the Elderly and Persons with Disabilities, 2004: 38).

International comparison data indicate that the employment rate among those aged 60 to 64 is 56.3%, and 38.7% among those aged 65 to 69 in Japan. Throughout the EU, such as Germany and France, the average employment rate is 23.5% for the former and 6.6% for the latter. This comparison shows that Japan is ranked high in the employment of elderly people (Japan Institute of Labour, 2000). In a recent survey of middle-aged people (40 - 59 years old), the subjects were asked about employment at the ages of between 65 and 69. Of them, 20.1% answered that they want to work everyday but will reduce their working hours, and 19.4% will work a few days a week. Although many desire to work in patterns other than full-time employment, about 70% of those surveyed have the intention to work. In addition, about 40% answered that they want to continue to work until the age of 70 (Japan Institute for Labour, 1998).

As the population ages, an increasing number of people continue to work over the long term in the post-retirement period. Against this backdrop, the establishment of a more flexible employment system has been facilitated to accommodate long-term career development among the senior age group. In particular, the baby-boomers enter their later stage of life in the near future. With a rapidly growing ageing population, it is necessary for Japan to establish a system that allows them to develop a wide variety of careers, taking advantage of their work or life experience (Yamaguchi and Kojima 2002). For this purpose, senior citizens should be considered as being in an "active ageing" generation and able to support society, not just "socially vulnerable."

With a rapidly ageing population and a changing employment system in mind, this chapter defines the post-retirement life stage as the second career-development period. In this chapter I examines the varied post-retirement career development, using various data. Bearing in mind that the compulsory retirement age does not mean retirement from work, the life stage ranging from the middle-aged years to the senior years is defined as the second career-development period, when people proactively pursue their careers, taking their retirement as an opportunity. Taking account of these perspectives written above, this chapter explores the varied post-retirement careers and lifestyle development.

2. Recent research directions

Before moving to explore this issue, research conducted so far concerning facts about employment in the later stage of life and senior workers' attitudes toward their careers should be mentioned. In recent years, policy discussions about post-retirement career development have been conducted mainly in terms of labor economics. For instance, Atsushi Seike put forward a theory about society with lifelong productivity. He claims that the mandatory retirement system should be abolished to extend the employment period, on the assumption that mandatory retirement could lead to age discrimination (Seike 1998). In experimental studies as well, many quantitative analyses have been examined, with the presence or absence of career choices as dependent variables, from the viewpoint of the "promotion of employment for the elderly (Okunishi 2001: 46)". Those studies in terms of labor economics have explored the possibility of extension of employment period in the later stage of life, anticipating the arrival of an era when Japan will have to confront a labor shortage due to demographic changes resulting from a falling birthrate.

Concerning career development in the post-retirement period, accumulated data are available in the areas of sociology and social gerontology. Shuichi Wada indicated early on that it is not unusual for retirees from companies to rejoin the labor force as full-time workers or business owners since forced retirement and actual retirement from the workforce can be considered different events under Japan's current employment system. Given the reality of the present retirement system in the country, he also noted that there are notable changes in career structure, resulting from mandatory retirement (Wada 1983a: 9). In the 1980s, he also showed occupational mobility patterns observed among retirees, based on detailed research data (Wada 1983a, 1983b). Kiyoko Okamura re-analyzed Wada's survey results, using the data of the survey conducted on retirees by the Tokyo Metropolitan Institute of Gerontology

(Okamura 1987). Findings from her re-analysis show that health performance is the most influential factor with which to determine whether senior workers remain in the labor force or not, though it also undeniably depends on how much pension they receive. Taking such knowledge into consideration, she concluded that in most cases, those in their early 60s tend to continue to work, but health problems and lack of job opportunities, rather than the size of pension, have driven them to leave the workforce. There are other detailed data analyses concerning such real-world situations of post-retirement employment (Aoi & Wada 1983, Ujihara 1985). Around the same time, U.S. research directions and theories concerning social gerontology were introduced into Japan (Sodei 1975, Wada 1983b).

In contrast, there have been few social studies conducted on the awareness of retirees. Against this background, Koichi Hiraoka carried out experimental studies in the 1980s (Hiraoka 1983). Out of samples collected in company surveys by Aoi and Wada (1983), he used the employee samples taken in 1978 with the subjects' mandatory retirement dates just around the corner, to perform an exhaustive quantitative analysis about their concerns about retirement, their image of post-retirement life, and their views about a mandatory retirement system. One of his findings is that employees whose retirement dates are near at hand tend not to have positive attitudes toward retirement. Many agreed with the view that some form of retirement system is necessary. However, they also shared fears about every aspect of their post-retirement life, and the mean value of their image of post retirement was not favorable (Hiraoka 1983: 169-70). Their worries about post-retirement life and negative attitudes toward retirement reflect the general image of retirement widely shared from the 1970s to 1980s. This experimentally verifies that most employees regarded a mandatory retirement system as a negative principle [1].

Thus, when taking a general view of studies about senior workers' employment and their views on their career, there are experimental studies proactively conducted in the realms of sociology and social gerontology, with particular emphasis on post-retirement career development patterns and their factor analyses. Now that elderly people are expected to remain in the work force over a prolonged period, however, this issue should be discussed from new, more in-depth perspectives.

Firstly, many past studies approached this issue in terms of economics, with focus on the extension of the mandatory retirement age and the abolishment of the retirement system. However, few discussed a post-retirement culture: how people define mandatory retirement. In particular, there have been few studies so far that have explored how a post retirement culture has been advanced in the history of Japanese society. Since the 1990s, considerable changes have taken place among businesses in their attitudes toward middle-to senior-age employees, as shown in the introduction of early retirement plans. However, many Japanese companies have applied the mandatory retirement system [2]. In studies on career development in the later stage of life, therefore, it is necessary to bring into focus from the sociological perspective the employees' views on retirement and the normative post-retirement culture shared among people, as well as the present state of company retirement policies.

Secondly, in most studies, analyses of occupational careers in the later stage of life focused on whether senior citizens are employed or unemployed. Few analyses have been conducted concerning the choices of post-retirement careers, ranging from participation in volunteer activities to the establishment of new businesses. It is true that senior citizens in Japan tend to be keen to find jobs and find fulfillment in their work. However, it is too early to conclude that work is their whole life. Some argue that in Japan, people have limited opportunities to participate in social activities, other than work, and the sense of fulfillment will be able to be maintained in the later stage of life as well if more opportunities to get involved in volunteer and other social activities are available (Wada 1988).

In reality, post-retirement lifestyles vary, and people are no longer forced to choose between extension of employment contracts and retirement. Now there is a wide choice of options for senior citizens, including paid or unpaid volunteer work in non-profit organizations and piecework, taking advantage of their accumulated expertise (The Japan Institute for Labour Policy and Training, 2004). Considering the current situations surrounding senior workers, it is necessary to define post-retirement career development as various patterns of a life course, including volunteer work and other non-economic activities as well as job continuation.

Thirdly, few studies have been performed about how career development in the later stage of life is correlated to employees' commitment to their companies. The idea that a retired man (husband) is naturally treated as *sodai gomi* (big waste) or *nure-ochiba* (gets underfoot at home) was once widely accepted. These terms were used to convey the sense of alienation that retired men, who placed great weight on their work in their life, have [3]. These days, however, an increasing number of employees keep some distance from the companies they work for, by actively interacting with those outside the company, improving occupational skills for self development and maintaining their prestige outside the company. Recent studies on employees' views and perceptions indicate that relatively fewer people find it attractive to become a "company-first" employee, represented by the "white-collar worker's image (Sato 2000). More employees have begun to think that living only for work is not an attractive prospect and they tend to find fulfillment through hobbies and other activities. In other words, there are growing tendencies to be involved in work and the companies they currently work for in a limited way only [4]. Under present conditions, post-retirement lifestyles and career choices are more likely to be affected by the level of commitment employees made while working for the company. In studies on occupational careers in the later stage of life, therefore, relationships between workers' commitment to the company they are currently working for and career choices after mandatory retirement should be investigated.

Thus far, previous researches have been reviewed and issues to be addressed in further studies were outlined. This chapter aims to throw some light on changes in post-retirement culture and corporate employees' attitudes toward career development in their latter stage of life. For this purpose, investigation will be carried out under three themes. Firstly, analysis is undertaken regarding male retirees' views on post-retirement life. Secondly, the attitudes of mid-career male workers in their late 30s to 50s are examined concerning post-retirement career development, including relationships between post-retirement career development and occupational autonomy, which is measured by the degree to which workers are committed to the companies they work for. Lastly, consideration is given to the advancement of post-retirement culture and active ageing, based on the results of the analyses.

3. Significance of mandatory retirement and occupational career

3.1 Current status of post-retirement career development

This section presents the results of an analysis of behavior and awareness concerning mandatory retirement, using data of nationwide surveys conducted on middle-to senior-age group [5]. In this paper, only male samples are used out of the data of three nationwide surveys carried out in 1991, 1996 and 2001.

First, consideration is given to the formation of occupational career. Table 2-1 shows the post-retirement career patterns of those already going through mandatory retirement, out of the all male samples in the three surveys conducted between 1991 and 2001. In the table, they are largely divided into three major groups. Type A represents retirement from the labor market: Type A1 shows those completely retiring from the workforce, and Type A2, those taking simple employment via temporary staff agencies for senior workers. Type

B shows a shift to the internal labor market after retirement: Type B1 represents those remaining on the payroll by renewing a job contract with their existing companies or getting rehired, and Type B2, those transferred to subsidiaries after retirement. Type C represents a shift to the external labor market: Type C1 shows those who re-enter the workforce by getting hired by other companies, and C2, those starting to run their own businesses after retirement.

Shown in the rightmost column in Table 2-1 are the total figures of post-retirement career patterns between 1991 and 2001. Ranked top is "job switch/re-employment" (33.6%), followed by "complete retirement from workforce" (23.4%) and "employment extension" (20.3%). Year-to-year comparisons of patterns of post-retirement career development between the years 1991 to 2001 show that the rate for "job switch/re-employment" decreased 7.4% (from 37.9% to 30.5%) and "employment extension" down 6.4% (from 23.9% to 17.5%). In contrast to the decline in "employment extension," "transfer to subsidiary" saw an increase from 13.5% to 16.6%, indicating the formation of quasi-internal labor market for companies by transferring employees to sub-

Table 2-1 Changes in Post-retirement Career Formation [†]

	1991	1996	2001	1991-2001(N)
A. Retirement from labor market				
A1: Complete retirement from workforce	17.6	24.7	27.5	23.4(577)
A2: Employment via temporary staff agency for senior workers	1.5	2.5	3.1	2.4(59)
B. Shift to the internal labor market				
B1: Employment extension	23.9	19.9	17.5	20.3(501)
B2: Transfer to subsidiary	13.5	13.5	16.6	14.6(360)
C. Shift to the external labor market				
C1: Job switch/re-employment	37.9	32.7	30.5	33.6(829)
C2: Establishment of new business/Self-employed	5.6	6.6	4.9	5.7(140)
Total	100.0	100.0	100.0	100.0
(N)	(800)	(785)	(881)	(2466)

[†] The subjects are all retired workers.

sidiaries during difficult economic times resulting from the burst of the economic bubble. The number of those "completely retired" from the labor market is on the increase (from 17.6% to 27.5%) [6]. The decade between 1991 and 2001 is often called the "second long-term economic slump" (Tominaga & Miyamoto 1998), when Japan saw the bursting of the bubble economy and a surge in unemployment. It is understood that during this period, employment conditions deteriorated, having a significant influence on the employment of the senior worker. These analysis results also reveal the worsening employment situations surrounding the elderly. Over the ten years, it can be said that senior workers saw a decrease in opportunities for extended employment after retirement and found it difficult to switch jobs or re-enter employment. It is also presumed that the employment of retirees was maintained largely by transferring them to subsidiaries.

3.2 Assessing the significance of mandatory retirement

How did workers' views on mandatory retirement change during the 1990s? Table 2-2 shows changes in the image of mandatory retirement over the decade. What is notable is that there were significant decreases in the number of people who believe that mandatory retirement means the "loss of title or an organization to belong to" (down 5.1% from 21.1% to 16.0%) and a "reduction in contact with people and access to information" (down 5.1% from 20.7% to 15.6%). In other words, fewer people have a negative image of mandatory retirement. In contrast, considerable increases were observed in the image of retirement as "making life financially difficult" (up 4.5% from 33.1% to 37.6%), "brings a lot of free time to enjoy oneself" (up 7.9% from 43.9% to 51.8%), and a "start point for a new life" (up 3.2% from 32.3% to 36.5%). Thus, there was a modest increase in the number of those worrying about finances in post-retirement life, but more people came to have a positive image, mentioning that retirement brings to them more time to enjoy them-

Table 2-2 Image of Mandatory Retirement† (%)

	1991 (N=2440)	1996 (N=2296)	2001 (N=2372)
<Positive image>			
Can be released from complex human relationships	27.4	26.2	25.1
Can spend more time with family	17.0	15.2	15.4
Can have more free time to enjoy oneself**	43.9	48.8	51.8
Can open up a new life**	32.3	33.3	36.5
Can be liberated from the same old routines	22.3	20.4	20.2
Can reduce mental stress	29.8	29.6	33.3
<Negative image>			
Lose title or organization to belong to**	21.1	19.0	16.0
Make life financially difficult**	33.1	35.3	37.6
Lose the objective of life or fighting spirit	18.4	16.1	14.9
Reduced contact with people or access to information**	20.7	22.9	15.6
Shut off from society	4.6	2.9	2.9
Lose means for self-fulfillment or chances	4.5	3.0	3.2

† The subjects are all men aged 35 to 74.
** Shows 4 points or more increase/decrease over the decade from 1991 to 2001.

selves. In short, mandatory retirement means a financial disadvantage, but more positively many regard retirement as an opportunity for career development in the later stage of their life. As shown in the decreased percentages of those concerned with the loss of title or of an organization to belong to, or a reduction in contact with people or access to information, more men consider themselves free from the traditional image of mandatory retirement and instead see retirement as an opportunity to open up a new life.

Then, how can these views on mandatory retirement be correlated to career development in later life? Tables 2-3(1) to 2-3(3) show the image of mandatory retirement by type of post-retirement career. According to Table 2-3(1), the rates of those answering it "makes life financially difficult" generally remained unchanged for the decade since 1991 in all types of post-retirement careers, except that there was a considerable decrease (from 58.3% to 29.6%) among those employed via temporary staff agencies.

Table 2-3(2) indicates that the image of retirement as "giving more time to enjoy oneself" is high among those "having employment contract extended" (up from 37.7% to 55.2%) and "transferred to subsidiary" (up from 46.3% to 63.0%). Most of all, a significant increase was observed among those "establishing new businesses/self employed (up from 33.3% to 65.1%)."

Table 2-3(3) shows that the percentage of those seeing retirement as "opening up a new life" are high among those establishing new businesses/self-employed (up 18.4% from 44.4% in 1991 to 62.8% in 2001. There was an upward surge (up 31.4% from 16.7% to 48.1%) among those employed via temporary staff agencies. What is notable in these analyses is that those leaving the workforce completely also have a positive image of mandatory retirement. In Table 2-3(3), for example, those answering "opening up a new life," among those completely retired from the labor market, is on a steady increase, up 6% from 30.5% in 1991 to 36.8% in 2001.

From these analyses to assess the significance of mandatory retirement by type of post-retirement careers, brought into focus are:

(1) The significance of mandatory retirement underwent changes over the 10 years from 1991 to 2001. Notably, there was a decline in negative significance, such as "loss of title/organization to belong to" and "reduction in contact with people or access to information."

(2) In contrast, the decade saw the emergence of value-conscious people, who define mandatory retirement as "giving more time to enjoy oneself" or "opening up a new life."

(3) Among those employed via temporary staff agencies for senior workers, there was a decrease in the image of "making life financially difficult," and there was an increase in the image of "opening up a new life."

(4) Those who established their own businesses or were self-employed showed the most positive attitudes toward mandatory retirement. In particular, they are high in the awareness that mandatory retirement "gives a

more free time to enjoy themselves" and "opens up a new life."

(5) Among those retiring from the workforce completely, the image that retirement "opens up a new life" shows an upward trend in the 1990s, therefore, it can be said that retirement is defined positively, not negatively, even by those already retired.

Although having a certain level of financial concern, senior workers have begun to view mandatory retirement as an opportunity to develop a new career, or open up a new life. In addition, there have been fewer concerns about loss of title and an organization to belong to as well as a reduction in concerns about loss of contact with people and access to information. This means that elderly workers are free from the old image of mandatory retirement as leaving the company and spending their last years in solitude. They now increasingly regard mandatory retirement not as a final goal, but rather as a vital transit point necessary for future career development in the course of a long life.

Table 2-3(1) Image of Post-retirement Life by Career Type† (%)

	\multicolumn{3}{c}{Image of post-retirement life "Makes life financially difficult"}
	1991 (N=800)	1996 (N=785)	2001 (N=881)
A1 Complete retirement from labor market**	26.2	24.2	20.7
A2 Employment via temporary staff agency for senior workers**	58.3	20.0	29.6
B1 Employment extension**	32.5	37.2	37.7
B2 Transfer to subsidiary**	27.8	35.8	34.2
C1 Job switch/re-employment	37.6	30.4	35.3
C2 Establishment of new businesses/Self-employed	20.0	28.8	23.3
Total	32.4	30.6	30.8

† The subjects are all men who went through mandatory retirement.
** Shows 4 points or more increase/decrease over the decade from 1991 to 2001.

Table 2-3(2) Image of Post-retirement Life by Career Type † (%)

	Image of post-retirement life "Can have more free time to enjoy oneself"		
	1991 (N=800)	1996 (N=785)	2001 (N=881)
A1 Complete retirement from labor market**	53.9	59.3	58.3
A2 Employment via temporary staff agency for senior workers**	41.7	55.0	48.1
B1 Employment extension**	37.7	39.1	55.2
B2 Transfer to subsidiary**	46.3	48.1	63.0
C1 Job switch/re-employment	42.2	51.4	46.1
C2 Establishment of new businesses/Self-employed	33.3	61.5	65.1
Total**	43.3	51.2	54.8

† The subjects are all men who went through mandatory retirement.
** Shows 4 points or more increase/decrease over the decade from 1991 to 2001.

Table 2-3(3) Image of Post-retirement Life by Career Type † (%)

	Image of post-retirement life "Can open up a new life"		
	1991 (N=800)	1996 (N=785)	2001 (N=881)
A1 Complete retirement from labor market**	30.5	37.1	36.8
A2 Employment via temporary staff agency for senior workers**	16.7	35.0	48.1
B1 Employment extension**	25.7	20.5	30.5
B2 Transfer to subsidiary**	38.0	34.9	37.7
C1 Job switch/re-employment**	28.7	31.1	33.1
C2 Establishment of new businesses/Self-employed**	44.4	51.9	62.8
Total**	30.3	32.5	36.3

† The subjects are all men who went through mandatory retirement.
** Shows 4 points or more increase/decrease over the decade from 1991 to 2001.

4. Intentions regarding post-retirement career development and occupational autonomy

4.1 Intentions regarding post-retirement career development

Next, an analysis is conducted of the relationship between post-retirement career development and occupational autonomy, using data of surveys held of middle-to and senior-age workers living in urban areas (Urban Area Survey)[7]. The samples used for analysis in this chapter are male workers aged 35 to 59 who have not yet gone through mandatory retirement, excluding those self-employed.

What do middle-aged men, or those in their late 30s to 50s, think about post-retirement life and career development? Table 2-4 shows their attitudes toward post-retirement career development[8]. As for the post-retirement career development, the subjects can be divided into three groups: retirement from the labor market, a shift to the internal labor market, and shift to the external labor market. The "retirement from labor market" can be further divided into three: complete retirement from the workforce, participation in volunteer activities (those intending to contribute to a local community and society by working for NPOs, NGOs or voluntary bodies), and employment via temporary staff agencies for senior workers" (those intending to get hired to handle simple tasks). The second category of "shift to the internal labor market" means "employment extension/transfer to subsidiary." In short, employees have their employment contract extended or are transferred to subsidiaries. The third category of "shift to the external labor market" consists of two groups: "job switch/re-

Table 2-4 Intention regarding Post-retirement Career Development†

	Frequency	%
A. Retirement from the labor market		
A1 Complete retirement from the workforce	81	19.2
A2 Participation in volunteer activities	28	6.7
A3 Employment via temporary staff agencies for senior workers	50	11.9
B. Shift to the internal labor market		
B1 Employment extension/transfer to subsidiary	100	23.8
C. Shift to the external labor market		
C1 Job switch/re-employment	99	23.5
C2 Establishment of a new business/self-employed	63	15.0
Total	421	100.0

† The subjects are all men aged 35 to 59 who have not yet gone through mandatory retirement.

employment" (those intending to enter a new company in their later life) and "establishment of a new business/self employed" (those wishing to start a business or become self-employed). Among those surveyed, ranked high are "employment extension/transfer to subsidiary" (23.8%), "job switch/re-employment" (23.5%), and "complete retirement from the workforce" (19.2%). In contrast, ranked low are "employment via temporary staff agencies for senior workers" (11.9%) and "participation in volunteer activities" (6.7%).

4.2 Occupational autonomy and intentions regarding post-retirement career development

Table 2-5 shows the relationship between the intentions of post-retirement career development among men and "occupational autonomy," [9] which represents a degree of dependence on their companies. The occupational autonomy was measured by six criteria: 1) actively interact with those outside the company, 2) plan for life predicated on long-term employment, 3) have something to be proud of outside the company, 4) personally develop vocational capability, 5) have done nothing special, and 6) prepare for job switch/establishing a new business. Three notable points were found here. The first is that the rate of those "planning their lives predicated on a long-term employment" is high in all career groups. Due consideration should be given to the data characteristic that shows subjects are living in urban areas, but the result indicates that many middle-aged corporate employees in Japan still intend to continue to work in the long term for the company they are currently working for [10].

The second point worth noting is the relationship between occupational autonomy and volunteer activities. The two criteria of "have something to be proud of outside the company" (75.0%) and "personally develop vocational capabilities" (71.4%) were rated higher among those with a desire for "participation in volunteer activities." Among those intending to "establish a new business," rated high are "actively interact with those outside the company"

Table 2-5 Occupational Autonomy and Intentions regarding Post-retirement Career Development†

(%)

(N)	Complete retirement from workforce	Participation in volunteer activities	Employment via temporary staff agencies for senior workers	Employment extension/ transfer to subsidiary	Job switch/ re-employment	Establishment of a new business	Total
	(79-81)	(28)	(49-50)	(100)	(98-99)	(63)	(419-421)
Actively interact with those outside the company	61.7	57.1	66.0	58.0	64.6	71.4	63.2
Plan for life predicated on lifelong employment	70.4	78.6	82.0	95.0	80.8	63.5	79.6
Have something to be proud of outside the company	64.2	75.0	54.0	66.0	57.1	69.8	63.3
Personally develop occupational capability	46.8	71.4	46.0	46.0	59.6	68.3	54.4
Have done nothing special	29.6	17.9	32.7	36.0	31.3	34.9	31.9
Prepare for job switch/ establishing a new business	25.9	50.0	24.5	17.0	39.4	66.7	34.5
Occupational autonomy score (total) [1)][2)]	9.26	10.18	8.58	8.12	9.05	10.94	9.17***

† The samples taken from Urban Area Data are all men aged 35 to 59 who have not gone through mandatory retirement.
Notes: 1) For the calculation of occupational autonomy scores in each criterion, three points were given to those choosing "Applicable," two points, "Somewhat Applicable," one point, "Not Very Applicable," and zero point, "Not Applicable." For the two of "plan for life predicated on lifelong employment" and "have done nothing special," the weights were reversed.
2) Based on mean difference in occupational autonomy scores. Level of significance ***<.01

(71.4%) and "personally develop vocational capabilities" (68.3%). On the other hand, "plan for life predicated on a long-term employment" was rated high among those intending to have "employment extension/transfer to subsidiary" (95.0%) and those intending to get "employed via temporary staff agencies for senior workers" (82.0%).

In short, those with higher occupational autonomy —those who do not rely on a lifelong employment system, have actively interacted with people outside the company, and have personally developed vocational capabilities— tend to express a higher intention to get involved in volunteer activities or establish a new business after retirement. In contrast, those planning their life predicated on long-term employment tend to have a desire to have their employment contract extended, get transferred to subsidiaries or get employed via temporary staff agencies for senior workers.

The third notable point is that the percentage of those having something to be proud of outside the company is considerably high among those having a desire to have their employment contract extended/be transferred to a subsidiary, as well as those intending to establish a new business. It can be assumed that the occupational autonomy has gradually increased even among workers largely depending on their companies for their life planning.

These results support the findings of recent research concerning the awareness of employees. (Sato 1999, Sato 2000) Therefore, it can be said that middle-aged employees are positive about long-term employment, while some of them tend to stop being "company-first employees" (Sato 2000), who devote their all energies to their company, before they retire.

Table 2-6 shows the logit analysis of occupational autonomy's impact on post-retirement career development, in which the variables of age, health conditions, and socio-economic status were controlled. This analysis indicates that for the type of "employment extension" the scores of age, annual household income and occupational autonomy are significant with variables at 5% or less.

In other words, those in their 40s or 50s have a stronger desire to continue to work for the company they are currently working for than those aged 39 or under. The same goes for those with lower annual household income and lower occupational autonomy scores. In short, corporate employees in a high age bracket who are low in annual household income and occupational autonomy are more likely to have their employment contract extended or re-enter the labor market after retirement.

Concerning the type of "volunteer activities," the two variables of "employment of wife" and "occupational autonomy" are significant. In other words, male workers whose wives are employed or those with high occupational autonomy have a greater likelihood of getting involved in volunteer activities. For those intending to "establish a new business," the two variables of the number of job switches (higher) and occupational autonomy are meaningful. Corporate employees with more job switches and higher occupational autonomy tend to have a desire to establish a new business or become self-employed.

These logit analysis results can be summarized as follows.
(1) In any career development type, occupational autonomy plays a significant role. It has a negative effect on those intending to continue to work for their companies. In contrast, it has a positive effect on those having a desire to get involved in volunteer activities or establish a new business. Therefore, occupational autonomy is a crucial factor that drives the diversification of career choices, other than employment extension.
(2) Some of independent variables in the logit analysis have significant effects on post-retirement career development. In the case of "employment extension," in particular, age has a more significant effect; the higher the age, the greater the significance. In this regard, the data used in this analysis were taken from the survey conducted at a certain point in time. It is difficult to distinguish whether the age-related results come from ageing or

Table 2-6 Logit Analysis of Intentions regarding Post-retirement Career Development †[4]

	Employment extension[1]		Volunteer activities[2]		Establishment of a new business[3]	
	β	EXP(β)	β	EXP(β)	β	EXP(β)
Age (vs. 39 or less)						
40 - 49	.568**	(1.764)	.000	(1.000)	.008	(1.108)
50 - 59	1.029***	(2.798)	.703	(2.020)	−.853*	(.426)
Health conditions (good)	.179	(1.197)	.003	(1.003)	−.002	(.998)
Academic background (vs. high school graduates)						
Vocational college/junior college	.577*	(1.781)	−17.9111	(.000)	.336	(1.399)
College/graduate school	.335	(1.398)	.710	(2.035)	.207	(1.230)
Current occupation (vs. managerial jobs)						
Specialist/engineer	.497	(1.643)	.682	(1.978)	−.392	(.676)
Desk job	.062	(1.064)	.414	(1.513)	.659	(1.933)
Sales/service/technician	.230	(1.259)	.352	(1.421)	.439	(1.551)
No. of job switches (high)	−.133*	(.875)	.003	(1.003)	.234***	(1.264)
Annual household income (high)	−.001***	(.999)	.001	(1.001)	.001	(1.001)
Employment status of wife (working wife)	.079	(1.082)	1.340**	(3.820)	−.289	(.749)
Occupational autonomy score (high)	−.105***	(.901)	.163**	(1.177)	.276***	(1.318)
Constant	.248	(1.282)	−6.877***	(.001)	−5.809***	(.003)
-2 Log Likelihood	554.684		161.303		270.172	
Model Chi-Square	27.495***		29.580***		43.237***	
N	431		431		431	

† The samples are 35- to 59-year-old workers, excluding the self-employed, who have no personal experience of mandatory retirement.
Notes: 1) The dummy variables of "1" and "0" were given to "continued employment" and others, respectively. The category of "employment extension" represents those intending to continue to work for the company they are working for: a combination of those intending to "have their employment contract extended/be transferred to a subsidiary" and those with a desire to "find a new job."
2) The dummy variables of "1" and "0" were applied to "volunteer activity" and others, respectively.
3) The dummy variables of "1" and "0" were applied to the type for "establishment of a new business" and others, respectively.
4) Level of significance *** < .01 ** < .05 * < .10

cohort influence. As shown in Table 2-1, however, a Nationwide Survey found that there was a considerable decrease during the decade from 1991 to 2001 in the number of retirees who have their employment extended by their companies after retirement. Given this, it can be assumed that cohort influences are found in the results of this logit analysis. In short, the cohorts of younger workers are more likely to have alternative career choices, such as running a new business and participation in volunteer activities, rather than employment extension. Another important finding is that the employment of the wife has a significant influence on the husband's choice of getting involved in volunteer activities. More men from the household where a working wife has made life financially affordable are expected to have a desire to get involved in volunteer activities after retirement. Thus, it can be said that a high economic level of a household is a crucial factor for men when they consider participation in volunteer activities during post-retirement life.

5. Conclusions and discussion

The purpose of the this chapter is to provide an insight into the factors behind a variety of post-retirement lifestyles and career developments, by defining the later stage of life as the second career development period, not as retirement from active life. This chapter concludes by describing some observations about lifestyles and career development in this later stage of life.

There are four observations. Firstly, there has been a change in the meaning of mandatory retirement. The percentage of those having the image of mandatory retirement as making life financially difficult increased in the 10 years from 1991, indicating that middle -aged people had been placed under a harsh employment situation. On the other hand, there was an increase in a positive image of retirement: it provides more free time to enjoy oneself, or the opportunity to open a new chapter on life. In this regard, a new post-retirement culture is now being created, in which mandatory retirement is regarded positively as being a vital turning point in a course of life and as the second stage of career development. A harsh employment environment characterized the period of the 1990s for workers. However, it was found that many people have positive attitudes toward mandatory retirement and have the intention to develop a variety of careers. Middle-aged employees were buffeted by the "lost decade" of the 1990s in terms of occupational career formation. However, they are contributing to the creation of a new post-retirement culture. Despite an economically difficult social environment - commonly known as the "second long-term economic slump" (Tominaga & Miyamoto 1998), middle-aged employees tend to regard mandatory retirement positively. What makes them so positive? After World War II, there was a considerable change in Japan in terms of demography: massive gains in life expectancy. Until the 1970s, people shared a traditional value of retirement, which could not catch up with demographic changes. The image of mandatory retirement as retirement from the labor market and active life had penetrated deeply into Japanese society. Recently, however, a new image of mandatory retirement has emerged. This is very different from the traditional post-retirement culture. It can be said that since the 1980s, a new post-retirement culture, in which mandatory retirement is viewed as a crucial turning point enabling the pursuit of career development has gradually replaced the old image.

The second concerns a variety of occupational career options following retirement. The career development of middle-aged employees who have not yet gone through official retirement tend to be influenced by financial conditions, such as whether the wife has a job and the amount of household income they have. A group of those with a desire to participate in volunteer activities after retirement are financially advantaged middle-aged people. Only 23% of the total show a desire to continue to work with the company they are currently working for or for a subsidiary, showing that the large percentage have a variety of choices in post-retirement career development, such as participation in volunteer activities and the establishment of new businesses.

Thirdly, the "occupational autonomy" to measure employees' devotion to their company is a driving factor behind a variety of career development choices. The analysis in this paper shows that the rate of those who answered that "they intend to plan their life predicated on long-term employment" was high in all types of post-retirement career choices. However, the items of "active interaction with those outside the company," "personal development of vocational capability," and "preparation for switching a job/establishing a new company" were mainly chosen by those with a desire to participate in volunteer activities or to establish a new business after retirement. This means that middle-aged people who have higher occupational autonomy and who place more emphasis on activities outside the company have a higher potential to regard mandatory retirement as an opportunity to pursue career development in various fields. Unlike those who want to continue to work for the company they are working for, those who intend to participate in volunteer activities or establish a new business after retirement start to search out a network of personal connections outside their companies before retirement. This can be called the individualism in occupational culture (Inagami 1992). The phenomenon to break away from the conventional mold of "company-first" employee has begun to cut across corporate employees, except for those who intend to continue to work for the company they are currently working for after mandatory retirement.

Lastly, one important implication is that due consideration should be given to post-retirement lifestyles and career development from the perspective of a diversity of life courses. In a social theory on a society with lifelong productivity, particular emphasis has been placed on the continuity of employment. However, it should be recognized that employment is just an alternative chosen from a variety of life-long career options, and that a wide range of career choices are available after retirement. It needs to be understood that active ageing is not only continuing to work as a member of a corporate structure. (Walker 1999). [11] Against this background, the Japanese government has promoted employment extension policies (Ministry of Health, Labour and Welfare, 1997). The policies should be promoted in a comprehensive manner by re-examining ways of working and the significance of working. With working for NPOs and establishing new businesses as an alternative from among a wide variety of options [12], the Japanese government should be called on to provide social support to make a variety of life courses available to its citizens.

Notes

[1] It is generally acknowledged that public awareness of mandatory retirement has changed considerably since the 1970s. For example, there are two essays of contrasting conclusions about the common image of retirement. In the 1970s, Seizo Okada described mandatory retirement as "social death" that takes place in the later stage of life in his book Teinen-go (The Life of Retirement under the Age Limit) (Okada 1976). This book describes how tragic corporate employees' life is, in which the date of retirement is called "retirement funeral," an adaptation of the funeral held after "biological death" that follows social death. The Japanese term *nure-ochiba-no-otto* (literal meaning: "wet-fallen-leaf husband") to depict a retired man who gets underfoot at home symbolizes what used to be the public reaction to mandatory retirement in those days. In contrast to the image of retirement provided by Okada, Oh! Teinen (Oh! Retirement), a book written by Jin Kato and published in the 1980s, defines post-retirement life as the starting point for a new life (Kato 1988). In this regard, refer to Amano (1999).

[2] According to the 2002 Employment Management Survey, only 8.5% of the companies surveyed across the nation do not adopt a retirement age system, and more than 90% do. Of the companies with a retirement age system, 96% have a uniform retirement system, 92.6% of which set mandatory retirement age at 60 to 64 (Japan Organization for Employment of the Elderly and Persons with Disabilities, 2004). Thus, many corporate employees in Japan need to go through mandatory retirement at a certain age.

[3] *Nureochiba* (literally means "wet-fallen-leaf") and *sodaigomi* (big waste) are negative terms used to depict a retired man who gets underfoot at home. Recently, post-retire-

ment life has started to be regarded as an "invaluable stage of life." In this regard, refer to (Iwanami Shoten Publisher. 1999: VI).

[4] This is also pointed out by Sato (1999). For details, refer to the findings of the survey conducted by the Policy Planning and Research Department, Minister's Secretariat, Ministry of Labour (1995).

[5] They are surveys conducted in 1991, 1996 and 2001 by Research Institute for Senior Life (2002). Male and female workers aged 35 to 74 and their spouses, who were enrolled in the Employees' Pension plan were the targets. Questionnaires were mailed to those selected from across the nation in a stratified random sampling method. The number of valid responses was 3,051 (76.3%) in the 1991 survey, 2,909 (70.2%) in the 1996 survey, and 3,189 (70.8%) in the 2001 survey. All samples used in the analysis were corporate employees prior to their retirement, who were enrolled in the Employees' Pension plan. Self-employed workers were not included in the analysis. Because of this, the percentage of those who had established a new business or were self-employed after retirement tend to be low, compared to standard samples collected from across the nation. In addition, consideration should be given to the fact that the subjects, who were enrolled in the Employees' Pension plan, tend to be in the higher earnings group with better working conditions than national-average workers.

[6] Changes in the post-retirement employment rate are largely attributable to the legally regulated mandatory retirement system. Following revisions in the Law for the Stabilization of Employment of the Aged in 1994, it was made mandatory for employees to retire workers at the age of 60. The revised law went into effect in 1998. When the 1991 and 1996 surveys in this paper were conducted, companies were being encouraged to promote the mandatory retirement at the age of 60, and the data show that the rate of those retiring from work before reaching 60 was high. The 2001 survey, however, indicates that many retired at the age of 60 or above. As a result, post-retirement employment rate is lower in 2001 than in 1991. For legal restrictions about the retirement system, refer to Nishimura (2004).

[7] Used were data of the survey conducted in 2003 by Research Institute for Senior Life on the diversity of employees' lifestyles and employment patterns. The subjects of the survey were 35 to 69 year-old male workers and their wives living in four prefectures (Tokyo, Kanagawa, Saitama and Chiba). In this survey, more detailed questions about employment conditions, family life, and social activities were added to the questionnaire used for the survey on corporate employees' life and purposes of life. The subjects were randomly selected from male workers living in the Tokyo metropolitan area, and questionnaires were posted to them. The number of valid responses was 875, or 43.8%.

[8] Post-retirement career development was measured by asking a question: "What do

you think will happen to your career after retirement?" A question could have been asked about their desire of a career. However, the above question was chosen in order to determine their career planning and intention from a realistic point of view.

[9] "Occupational autonomy" can be defined as "employees' attitudes that do not overly depend on the company but control their own occupational career in a positive way" (Honda 1998), namely, the behavioral characteristic that employees personally participated in, such as vocational training programs or the obtaining of qualifications for career improvement, while keeping a certain distance from the company they work for. They place emphasis on the values of not belonging to organizations. In other words, they have a self-oriented attitude toward their career, not an organization-oriented attitude resulting from strong commitments to the company they work for. In this regard, this is the opposite of the conventional idea that company-oriented workers have supported Japan's employment system. For manipulated variables, refer to Maeda (2003) and Ikeda (2003).

[10] Even during the recession from the 1990s onward, a life-employment system has not collapsed for many employees. Takeshi Inagami indicates that under the Heisei Recession, many middle-aged white-collar employees were transferred forcibly to subsidiaries or undertook a change in employment, but in reality manipulation of the labor market by business groups or the formation of a quasi-internal labor market brought about the creation of a lifetime employment zone (Inagami 1999). A recent survey on the awareness of employees shows that employees' awareness of "lifetime employment" and a "sense of belonging" has not been diminished compared to 20 years ago. On the other hand, an increasing number of men in their 50s and 60s favor self-help capability development, indicating that Japanese-style employment is now facing challenges to better "balance traditional values and innovation" (The Japan Institute for Labour Policy and Training, 2004).

[11] Alan Walker notes that unlike the term "productive ageing" used in the US, the term "active ageing" covers a wide-ranging concept, including active roles played in other places than the labor market (Japan Institute of Labour, 2001: 359). For the US situation, refer to Rix (2001), and for European conditions, see de Vroom and Guillemard, A (2002).

[12] Taking their physical strength and lifestyles into account, non-regular employment of those in the later stage of life can be positively evaluated within various working patterns. For relations between atypical employment and life, refer to Maeda (2000, 2002).

Transition to Later Life and Life Planning

Chapter 3

1. Transition to later life

In rapidly ageing Japan, the raising of the age at which pensions are payable and with employment extended from 60 to 65 have been placed on the political agenda, and lively discussions have been made regarding employment in later life. In considering an employment system for older people, the important point is what working patterns are desirable to workers who enter the later stage of life and what lifestyles they intend. With males aged 40 to 59 as the subjects, this chapter analyses their future life plans and willingness to work.

Compared to other countries, Japan is high in the employment rate of those in later life. For example, 2002 statistics show that the employment rate of males aged 60 to 64 stands at 70.9% in Japan, surpassing 33.3% in Germany, 16.3% in France and 57.6% in the U.S (Japan Organization for Employment of the Elderly and Persons with Disabilities, 2004). In France, Germany and other European countries, some people enter retirement before the age of 60 partly due to active implementation of early retirement policies. In contrast, Japanese people have a strong willingness to work in later life, partly because of the country's high self-employment rate. Then, will the employment rate of elderly people remain high in the future? If such a high employment rate is maintained, what is the driving force behind elderly people's intention to work? To address these questions, this chapter analyses Japanese males aged 40 to 59, who have not yet reached the later stage of life, to determine their life plans and willingness to work in later life. There are some studies about willingness to work in later life and its determinant factors, but this chapter brings into focus three factors that could have influences on willingness to work and life planning in later life. The first is financial, including income, mortgage and savings. The second is life-course factors, such as a birth cohort, first-marriage age and the age of having the youngest child. The third is occupational career factors, like academic background, employment status and willingness to go into self-employment. With focus on these three factors, the reason why middle-aged males show a strong desire to work in later life is examined.

2. Life planning and willingness to work

To begin, a brief examination is given to the willingness to work and life planning in later life of males aged 40 to 59 [1]. In the study, they were asked about their life design at the three ages of 60-64, 65-69 and over 70.

Figure 3-1 shows their life plans at the age 60-64. Only 8.0% said that they will live on their pensions/savings without working. Most people plan to continue to work in some form, and the highest percentage (26.5%) think that they will have a full-time job at a company. Meanwhile, 25.3% answered that they will reduce working hours per day, demonstrating a desire for short-time work. Those planning to become self-employed/start business and those wishing to work under a contract form without time constraints represent 18.7% and 11.2% respectively. Thus, those planning to remain in the workforce in later life vary in working patterns.

Concerning their life planning at the age of 65-69 (Fig. 3-2), 30.3% said that they will live on their pensions/savings without working, and the rest of the males surveyed plan to continue to work in some form. A breakdown of those planning to remain in the labor market is: 3.8% desire to "work full-time

Transition to Later Life and Life Planning   49

at a company," 20.1% "reduce work time per day," 19.4% "work only a few days a week," and 17.9% "work under a contract form, without time constraints." These results indicate increasingly diversified patterns of work.

Figure 3-3 shows the life plans of the subjects after the age of 70. Of the total, 60.5% said that they will live on their pensions/savings. Approximately 60% of those surveyed think they will leave the labor market after the age of

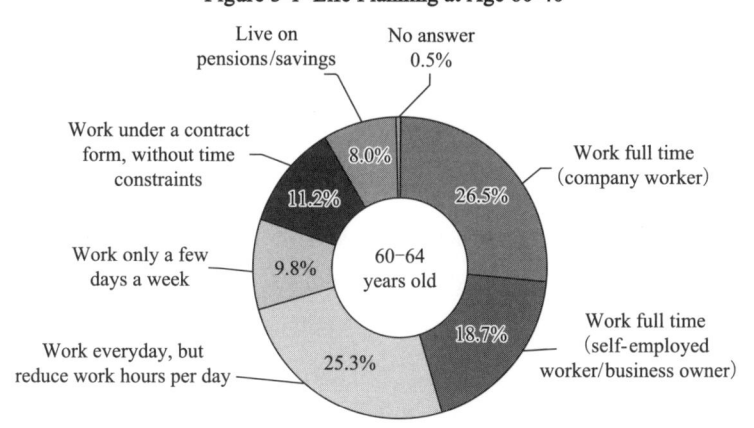

Figure 3-1 Life Planning at Age 60-40

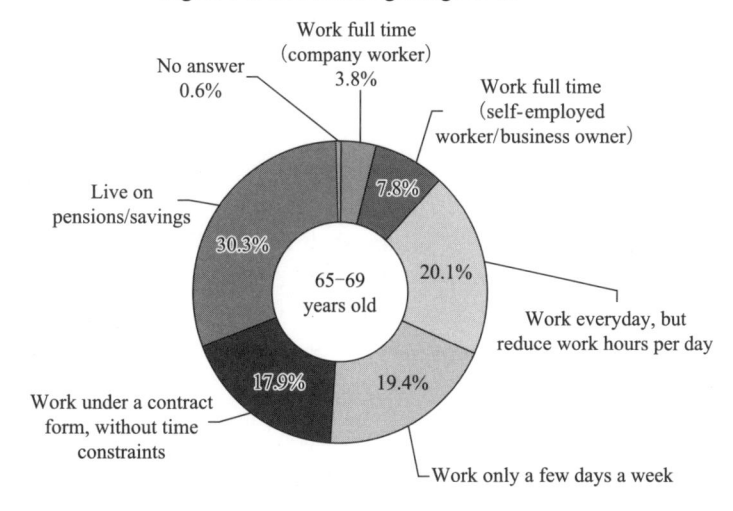

- Live on pensions/savings: 8.0%
- No answer: 0.5%
- Work full time (company worker): 26.5%
- Work full time (self-employed worker/business owner): 18.7%
- Work everyday, but reduce work hours per day: 25.3%
- Work only a few days a week: 9.8%
- Work under a contract form, without time constraints: 11.2%

(60–64 years old)

Figure 3-2 Life Planning at Age 65-69

- No answer: 0.6%
- Work full time (company worker): 3.8%
- Work full time (self-employed worker/business owner): 7.8%
- Work everyday, but reduce work hours per day: 20.1%
- Work only a few days a week: 19.4%
- Work under a contract form, without time constraints: 17.9%
- Live on pensions/savings: 30.3%

(65–69 years old)

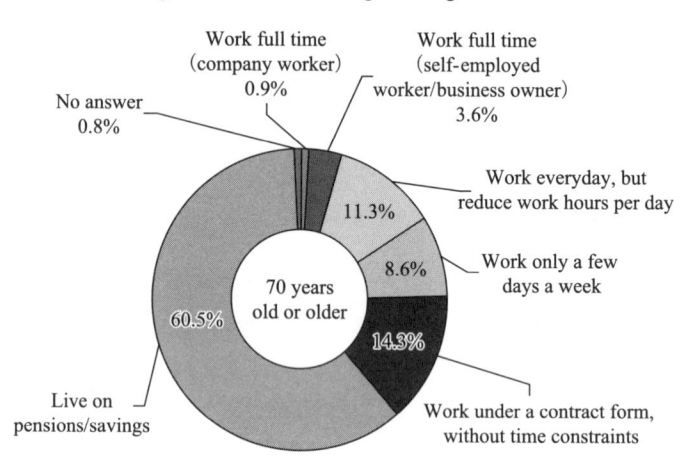

Figure 3-3 Life Planning after Age 70

- Work full time (company worker) 0.9%
- Work full time (self-employed worker/business owner) 3.6%
- No answer 0.8%
- Work everyday, but reduce work hours per day 11.3%
- Work only a few days a week 8.6%
- 70 years old or older
- Live on pensions/savings 60.5%
- Work under a contract form, without time constraints 14.3%

70. However, the remaining 40% have a desire to work in some form. Of them, the highest percentage answered that they will "work under a contract form, without time constraints" (14.3%), which is followed by "work every day, but reduce work time per day" (11.3%). Thus, those who have a desire to continue to work after the age of 70 accounts for nearly 40%, indicating that the middle-aged people surveyed have a substantially high willingness to work in later life.

The next question is: what contributing factors are there to support such a high willingness to work? The reason why the middle-aged males have such a high desire to work is examined from three perspectives: (1) mortgage and other financial factors, (2) marriage age and other life-course factors, and (3) occupational career-related factors, such as a willingness to become self-employed/start business.

3. Contributing factors to willingness to work

3.1 Assets/mortgage and willingness to work

As indicated in Fig. 3-3, a large proportion of middle-aged males have a willingness to work even after the age of 70. This is examined in terms of economic burden. Figure 3-4 is a diagram illustrating the distribution of the respondents having a desire to work after the age of 70 by the amount of mortgage loan outstanding. Those having a mortgage loan outstanding of less than ￥5 million indicate the lowest willingness to work after the age of 70, representing 19.4%. In contrast, the higher the amount of mortgage outstanding, the higher the willingness to work. For example, 35.7% of those having a mortgage outstanding of more than ￥10 million to ￥15 million said that they want to continue to work after reaching 70 years old. Among those with more than a ￥15 million mortgage, the figure increases to 47.4%. Obviously, the amount of mortgage loan affects willingness to work after the age of 70.

Next, Fig. 3-5 indicates the relation between the age of paying off a mortgage loan and willingness to work. It is also found that the age in which they

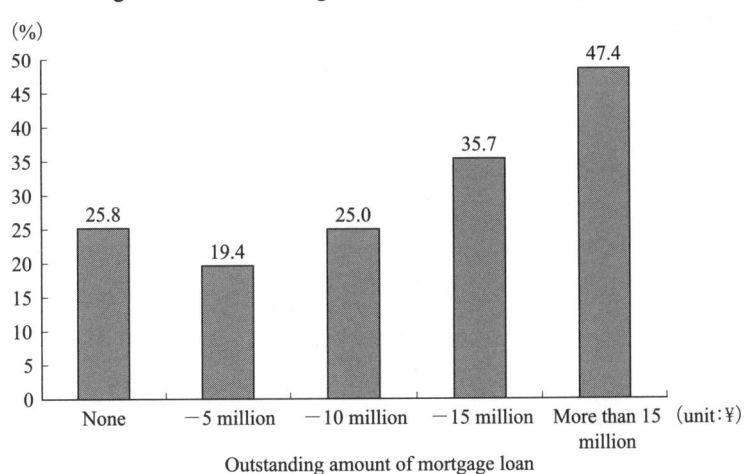

Figure 3-4 Have Willingness to Work after after Age 70

(%)

Outstanding amount of mortgage loan	%
None	25.8
−5 million	19.4
−10 million	25.0
−15 million	35.7
More than 15 million	47.4

(unit：￥)

Figure 3-5 Have Willingness to Work after after Age 70

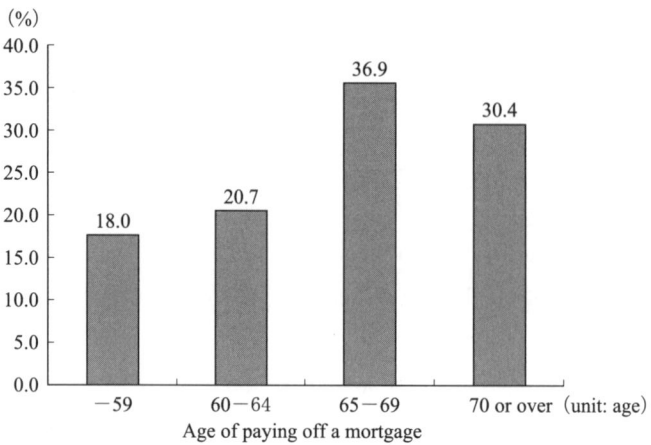

```
(%)
40.0
35.0                        36.9
30.0                                   30.4
25.0
20.0           20.7
      18.0
15.0
10.0
 5.0
 0.0
       -59    60-64    65-69   70 or over  (unit: age)
              Age of paying off a mortgage
```

Figure 3-6 The Desired Age until Which to Remain in the Workforce

- Birth cohort: age 55-59
- Desired age until which to remain in the workforce: age 67.3
- Amount of mortgage outstanding: more than ¥15 million
- House purchase on one's own

Age 67.3 > 64.8 (total sample)

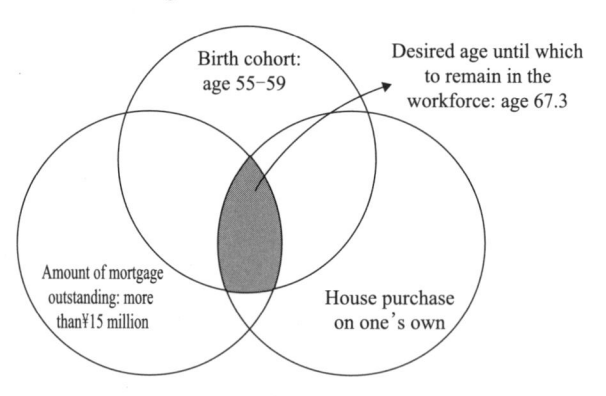

pay off their mortgage loans influences the willingness to work after the age of 70. Of those who are to pay off a mortgage by the age of 59, 18.0% show a desire to work after 70. However, the figure significantly increases when a mortgage is due to be paid off at 65 or over. In particular, as much as 36.9% of those who are to repay a mortgage loan at the age of between 65 and 69 answered they wish to continue to work after 70.

As stated, the economic burden of a mortgage loan has an obvious effect on willingness to work in later life. Figure 3-6 indicates the combined influences of the three factors - "birth cohort," "outstanding amount of mortgage," and "house purchase on one's own - on the desired age until which to remain in the workforce. The average of the desired age until which to remain in the workforce of the total sample is 64.8 years old. For those who are in the birth cohort of age 55-59 [2], have mortgage outstanding of ¥15 million, and purchased their houses on their own, however, it increases to 67.3 years old, two years longer than the average desired age until which to continue working. Therefore, it can be said that economic factors to build up assets, such as to own a house through a mortgage, affect middle-aged males' future working patterns.

3.2 Life course and willingness to work

In this section, life-course factors contributing to willingness to work in later life is examined. There are some possible life-course factors, but an approach is made here from the two perspectives of a "birth cohort" and the "age of having the youngest child." The term "birth cohort" here indicates a group of people who were born in the same year, which is represented by the age of the subjects as of 1996, when a survey to collect the data used for this chapter was conducted.

Figure 3-7 indicates the percentage of people who have a willingness to work after the age of 70 by birth cohort. Of all cohorts, the birth cohort of age 40-44 showed the lowest willingness to work after the age of 70 at 20.7%. In contrast, 29.3% of the birth cohorts of age 55-50 say the same thing, which is higher than any other birth cohort. Because this is a survey that looks at a cross-section of a group at one point in time, it is hard to differentiate between generation effects and age effects. As far as this analysis is concerned, the cohort of age 55-59 indicates more willingness to work in later life. This can be attributed to two factors. Firstly, it reflects their realization that the mandatory retirement age of 60 is just around the corner. Secondly, more people in older birth cohorts tend to show more commitment to the company they work for, making them feel like more work in later life. Based on the latter interpretation, people in younger cohorts are expected to have a lower commitment to work, thereby leading to lower willingness to work in later life

The next analysis determines what effects the age of having the youngest child has on willingness to work. Table 3-1 indicates the desired age to leave the workforce by the age of having the youngest child. In the cohort of males aged 40 to 44, the desired retirement age of those having the youngest child at the age of 29 or under is 63.67, while the figure rises to 65.96 among those begetting the youngest child at the age of 30 to 34. In the cohort of males aged 45 to 49, the desired retirement age is 64.19 for those fathering the youngest child at the age of 29 or below, 64.60 for those begetting the youngest child at the age of 30 to 34, and 65.24 for those having the youngest child after the age of 35. Thus, the higher the age of fathering the youngest child is, the higher the desired retirement age. This is true of the cohorts of males aged 50 to 54 and 55 to 59, demonstrating the same tendency in any cohort that males who had

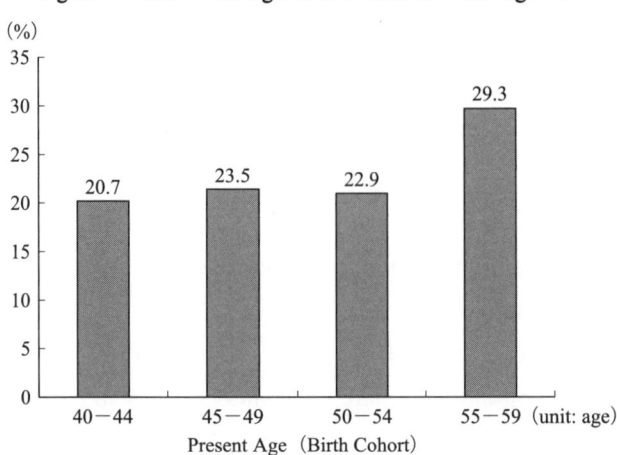

Figure 3-7 Have Willingness to Work after after Age 70

Present Age (Birth Cohort)	%
40−44	20.7
45−49	23.5
50−54	22.9
55−59	29.3

(unit: age)

Table 3-1 Desired Retirement Age by the Age of Having the Youngest Child in Each Birth Cohort

Cohort: Age 40 – 44	
Age of having youngest child	Desired retirement age
29 or below	63.67
30 – 34	65.96
35 or over	64.10
Cohort: Age 45 – 49	
Age of having youngest child	Desired retirement age
29 or below	64.19
30 – 34	64.60
35 or over	65.24
Cohort: Age 50 – 54	
Age of having youngest child	Desired retirement age
29 or below	63.41
30 – 34	65.00
35 or over	65.04
Cohort: Age 55 – 59	
Age of having youngest child	Desired retirement age
29 or below	64.97
30 – 34	66.39
35 or over	66.42

the youngest child later want to leave the workforce later. Therefore, it can be concluded that the later the males had the youngest child, the later they leave the labor market even in the later stage of life.

3.3 Intention to become self-employed/start a business and willingness to work

This section examines what influences the future career possibilities have on willingness to work in later life. In particular, focus is placed on how the desired retirement age changes when employed workers (corporate employees) have the intention of becoming self-employed or starting a business. Table 3-2 provides the desired retirement age by the future occupational career desired.

In the table, the term "employed to employed" means that the surveyed who are currently corporate employees wish to remain employed workers. The term "employed to self-employed" indicates that those currently working for a company have a desire to start a business. The term "self-employed to self-employed" is for the self-employed who wish to remain self-employed. The "self-employed to employed" means that those who are currently self-employed want to be corporate workers in the future. This analysis shows that the desired retirement age of the "employed to employed" group is 64.19, while that of the "employed to self-employed" is 65.72. It is evident that those intending to become self-employed/start a business have more willingness to work in later life. In Japan, the level of willingness to work of elderly people is generally proportional to the nation's ratio of self-employed. Since the self-employed tend to leave the workforce later than corporate employees, it is said that Japan with a high rate of the self-employed is high in the employment rate of older people. This analysis indicates that people in the occupational career pattern of "self-employed to self-employed" are the latest in leaving the labor market (67.43 years old). At the same time, those in the "employed to self-employed" pattern also tend to desire late retirement (65.72 years old). Accordingly, it can be estimated that the intention of becoming self-employed/starting a business is an important factor to enhance the willingness to work in later life.

Furthermore, some analyses are carried out here with focus on the "employed to self-employed" group, who has a strong intention of becoming

Table 3-2 Desired Retirement Age by the Future Occupational Career Desired

Occupational Career	Desired Retirement Age
Employed to employed	64.19
Employed to self-employed	65.72
Self-employed to self-employed	67.43
Self-employed to employed	64.81

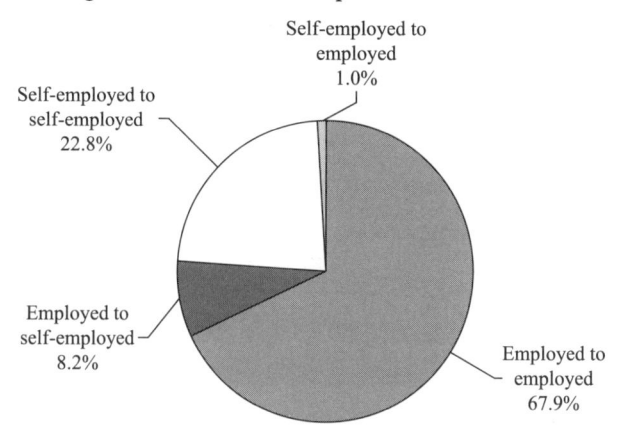

Figure 3-8 The Future Occupational Career Desired

- Self-employed to employed 1.0%
- Self-employed to self-employed 22.8%
- Employed to self-employed 8.2%
- Employed to employed 67.9%

self-employed/starting a business. Figure 3-8 shows the future occupational career patterns the surveyed desire. The ratio of the "employed to employed" pattern accounts for 67.9% of the total, followed by "self-employed to self-employed" (22.8%), "employed to self-employed" (8.2%) and "self-employed to employed" (1.0%). Then, what drives people to have the desire to become self-employed/start a business?

Table 3-3 provides the future occupational career desired by birth cohort. What is notable here is that the rate of "employed to self-employed" is higher in younger birth cohorts. In the cohort of age 50-54, 8.9% have the intention of becoming self-employed, 4.4% in the 55-59 cohort, and 11.3% in the 40-44 cohort, indicating that those in younger cohorts show a stronger desire to

Table 3-3 Future Occupational Career Desired by Birth Cohort (% (N))

	Employed to employed	Employed to self-employed	Self-employed to self-employed	Self-employed to employed	Total
Age 40–44 cohort	71.2 (158)	11.3 (25)	17.1 (38)	0.5 (1)	100.0 (222)
Age 45–49 cohort	67.2 (225)	8.7 (29)	22.1 (74)	2.1 (7)	100.0 (335)
Age 50–54 cohort	65.9 (170)	8.9 (23)	24.0 (62)	1.2 (3)	100.0 (258)
Age 55–59 cohort	68.1 (171)	4.4 (11)	27.5 (69)	0.0 (0)	100.0 (251)
Total	67.9 (724)	8.3 (88)	22.8 (243)	1.0 (11)	100.0 (1,066)

become self-employed/start a business.

Table 3-4 provides the future occupational career desired by academic background. In the "employed to self-employed" pattern, those with a higher academic background tend to have a stronger desire to become self-employed/start a business in later life. Of junior high school graduates, 3.6% have the intention to change from corporate employees to self-employed workers, 6.4% of high school graduates, and 11.6% of college graduates. It is evident that the higher the academic background they have, the stronger the desire to become self-employed/start a business. Table 3-5 indicates the future occupational career desired by occupation. More intention to become self-

Table 3-4 Future Occupational Career Desired by Academic Background (% (N))

	Employed to employed	Employed to self-employed	Self-employed to self-employed	Self-employed to employed	Total
Junior high school graduates	53.9 (89)	3.6 (6)	41.2 (68)	1.2 (2)	100.0 (165)
High school graduates	72.4 (304)	6.4 (27)	20.0 (84)	1.2 (5)	100.0 (420)
Junior college/vocational school graduates	56.3 (58)	10.7 (11)	31.1 (82)	1.9 (2)	100.0 (103)
College graduates or higher	72.4 (275)	11.6 (44)	15.5 (59)	0.5 (2)	100.0 (380)
Total	68.0 (726)	8.2 (88)	22.8 (243)	1.0 (11)	100.0 (1,068)

Table 3-5 Future Occupational Career Desired by Occupation (% (N))

	Employed to employed	Employed to self-employed	Total
Specialists/engineers	85.9 (134)	14.1 (22)	100.0 (156)
Managerial position	89.9 (204)	10.1 (23)	100.0 (227)
Clerical staff	90.1 (91)	9.9 (10)	100.0 (101)
Sales	85.6 (89)	14.4 (15)	100.0 (104)
Service	92.9 (39)	7.1 (3)	100.0 (42)
Security-related	94.7 (18)	5.3 (1)	100.0 (19)
Transportation/communications	91.9 (57)	8.1 (5)	100.0 (62)
Skilled workers/laborers	90.9 (90)	9.1 (9)	100.0 (99)
Total	89.1 (722)	10.9 (88)	100.0 (810)

employed/start a business is observed among specialists/engineers and those engaged in sales.

Next, the relation between the lifestyle of workers and the intention to become self-employed/start a business is examined. Tables 3-6 and 3-7 show social (communal) activities of the workers surveyed. Table 3-6 presents the actual conditions of their social (communal) activities.

It is noteworthy that in the "employed to self-employed" group, a high proportion of people have spent time on social (communal) activities, which is more pronounced when compared to those in the "employed to employed" group. In the "employed to self-employed" group, 10.2% said that they have spent a lot of time on social (communal) activities, far surpassing the 4.5% of

Table 3-6 Involvement in Social (Communal) Activities by the Future Occupational Career Desired (% (N))

	Spend a lot of time + spend considerable time	Spend a certain amount of time	Not spend much time + spend no time	Total
Employed to employed	4.5 (32)	14.7 (104)	80.8 (573)	100.0 (709)
Employed to self-employed	10.2 (9)	11.4 (10)	78.4 (69)	100.0 (88)
Self-employed to self-employed	7.9 (19)	26.7 (64)	65.4 (157)	100.0 (240)
Self-employed to employed	10.0 (1)	30.0 (3)	60.0 (6)	100.0 (10)
Total	5.8 (61)	17.3 (181)	76.9 (805)	100.0 (1,047)

The current involvement level in social (communal) activitie

Table 3-7 Future Involvement in Social (Communal) Activities by the Future Occupational Career Desired (% (N))

	Give a lot of importance + give considerable importance	Give a certain amount of importance	Not give much importance + give no importance	Total
Employed to employed	7.5 (54)	40.2 (288)	52.3 (375)	100.0 (717)
Employed to self-employed	12.5 (11)	44.3 (39)	43.2 (38)	100.0 (88)
Self-employed to self-employed	9.5 (23)	45.3 (110)	45.3 (110)	100.0 (243)
Self-employed to employed	10.0 (1)	50.0 (5)	40.0 (4)	100.0 (10)
Total	8.4 (89)	41.8 (442)	49.8 (527)	100.0 (1,058)

The future involvement level in social (communal) activities the "employed to employed" group. It can be supposed that the level of involvement of present corporate workers in social activities, such as volunteer activities is affected by whether they have the intention of becoming self-employed/starting a business or not.

Consideration is also given to the relation between the future involvement of the males surveyed in social (communal) activities. Table 3-7 shows that 7.5% of the "employed to employed" group answered that they will "give a lot of importance + give considerable importance," whereas 12.5% of the "employed to self-employed" group said the same thing. It is clear that the corporate workers who have more desire to become self-employed/start a business tend to have more willingness to get involved in social activities. In Table 3-7, 9.5% of the "self-employed to self-employed" group said that they will "give a lot of importance + give considerable importance" to social (communal) activities in the future, which is lower than the "self-employed to employed" group. Thus, those who are currently corporate employees and have the intention of becoming self-employed/starting a business tend to be more involved in social activities or have more willingness to do so in the future. As shown in the tendency that the subjects as a whole give less importance to social activities, the fact that Japanese males "place more emphasis on work and attach less importance to social (communal) activities" is brought into sharp relief. However, the data suggest that willingness to become self-employed/start a business contributes to the promotion of social activities.

In the above, it was confirmed that corporate workers' desire to become self-employed/start a business tends to heighten their willingness to work in later life. And, a stronger desire to become self-employed/start a business has been observed in younger cohorts. Those with a better educational background and those engaged in a special line of work or sales tend to show more willingness to go into business for themselves. Furthermore, it has been determined that such a desire is connected to the willingness to get involved in social activities, and that corporate workers' intention of becoming self-employed and starting a business helps promote their involvement in volunteer and other social activities.

4. Logit analysis of willingness to work in later life

In this section, willingness to work in later life is examined by logit analysis and multiple regression analysis. In logit analysis, the influence of some independent variables at a given age is estimated on the dummy variables of "1" and "0," which are applied to "taking a job" and "not taking a job" respectively. In multiple regression analysis, desired retirement age is used as dependent variables to measure the influence of some independent variables. In carrying out logit analysis and multiple regression analysis, special attention is paid to three independent variables. The first is the "asset/economic variables." They are the three variables of mortgage, savings and income. In the case of mortgage, the dummy variables of "1" and "0" are applied to the amount of mortgage outstanding of less than ¥15 million and over ¥15 million, respectively. For savings, the codes of "0," "1" and "2" are given to "no savings," "less than ¥1 million" and "¥1 million to 2 million" respectively, and in total the continuous variables of zero to nine were used. For incomes, less than ¥10 million is expressed in categorical variables from "¥250,000," "¥500,000" to "¥9.5 million," which are transformed into real values with continuous valuables of ¥0 to ¥9.99 million. The second independent variable group is "occupational career and the intention of becoming self-employed/starting a business." They include the three variables of "academic background," "employer dummy," and the "intention of becoming self-employed/starting a business." With regard to academic background, the code "1" is used for "junior high school graduates," "2" for "high school graduates," "3" for "junior college/vocational school graduates," and "4" for "college graduates or higher." For the employer dummy variables, "0" and "1" are applied to the "self-employed" and "corporate workers," respectively. Regarding the "intention of becoming self-employed/starting business," the "employed to the self-employed" category was transformed "1," and the other, "0." The third independent variable group is "life course," which consists of four variables: "birth cohort," "marriage age," the "age of having the youngest child," and the "number of children." For these variables, real values are applied as continuous variables.

Table 3-8 provides the results of logit analysis concerning the presence or absence of willingness to work in the future. The analysis was performed with the presence or absence of willingness to work at the three ages of 60-64, 65-69 and 70 or over transformed to dependent variables. The influence of independent variables on the presence/absence of willingness to work at the age of

Table 3-8 Logit Analysis on Future Willingness to Work

	Presence/Absence of Willingness to Work		
	Age 60-64 β EXP(β)	Age 65-69 β EXP(β)	Age 70+ β EXP(β)
Birth cohort	−.0400 (.9607)	.0196 (1.0171)	−.0850 (.9185)
Academic background	−.3625 (.6959)	.1103 (1.1166)	.0883 (1.0923)
Employer dummy	.6905 (1.9948)	1.3245 (3.7602)	−.2717 (.7621)
Intention of becoming self-employed/starting business	1.1447 (3.1416)	2.0603 (7.8485)*	1.4108 (4.0994)*
Income	−.0014 (.9986)**	−.0002 (.9998)	.0005 (1.0005)
Marriage age	−.1713 (.8426)	−.0105 (.9896)	−.0321 (.9684)
Age of having the youngest child	.4575 (1.5801)**	.0904 (1.0946)	.0773 (1.0804)
No. of children	−.5139 (.5982)	.0184 (1.0186)	−.7325 (.4807)*
Mortgage	.6093 (1.8391)	−.2151 (.8064)	−.2280 (.7961)
Savings	.0002 (1.0002)	7.46E-05 (1.0001)	−.0004 (.9996)*
Constant	−4.2297	−5.6229	2.8334
−2 Log Likelihood	59.198	136.369	124.490
Model Chi-square	12.943	7.941	18.420**
N	113	113	113

Note: Significant level ***<.01 **<.05 *<.10

60-64 is significant in "income ($\beta = -.0014$)" and the "age of having the youngest child ($\beta = .4575$)." In short, those with higher incomes are significantly lower regarding the possibility of employment at the age of 60-64. In contrast, it was found that the possibility of employment at the age of 60-64 gets significantly higher for those who had the youngest children at a later age. Concerning the effect of independent variables on the presence/absence at the age of 65-69, significant influences were observed in the "intention of becoming self-employed/starting a business ($\beta = 2.0603$)." The stronger the intention of becoming self-employed/starting a business, the significantly higher the possibility of employment at the age of 65-69 is. Furthermore, consideration is given to the effects of independent variables on the presence/absence of employment at the age of 70 or over. Significant values were displayed in three variables: the "intention of becoming self-employed/starting business ($\beta = 1.4108$)," "no. of children ($\beta = -.7325$)" and "savings ($\beta = -.0004$)." This indicates that those with a stronger desire to become self-employed/start business tend to have more willingness to work after the age of 70. In contrast, the more children or savings they have, the lower the willingness to work after the age of 70 they show. This logit analysis has clearly disclosed that future willingness to work of those in their early 60s is considerably affected by when they had the youngest child, and for those aged 65 or over, it is highly influenced by whether they have the intention of becoming self-employed/starting a business. The same results were also observed in the next multiple regression analysis. Table 3-9 provides the results of multiple regression analysis with desired retirement ages (real values) used as dependent variables. In this analysis, the two variables of the "intention of becoming self-employed/starting a business is significant ($\beta = .3222$)" and the "age of having the youngest child ($\beta = .3070$)." This shows that the desired retirement age rises when they have a desire to become self-employed/start a business or when they had the youngest child at a later age. Therefore, the logit analysis and multiple regres-

Table 3-9 Multiple Regression Analysis on Desired Retirement Age

	Desired retirement age
	regression coefficient (t-value)
Birth cohort	.0937 (.674)
Academic background	.0988 (1.031)
Employer dummy	.1386 (.937)
Intention of becoming self-employed/starting a business	.3222 (2.061)**
Income	−.0263 (−.261)
Marriage age	−.1425 (−.997)
Age of having the youngest child	.3070 (1.966)*
No. of children	−.1118 (−.756)
Mortgage	−.0899 (−.812)
Savings	.0155 (.149)
Adj. R^2	.0431
Sig. F	.1486
N	113

Note: Significant level ***<.01 **<.05 *<.10

sion analysis, with other variables controlled, indicate that the two variables of the "intention of becoming self-employed/starting a business" and the "age of having the youngest child" have significant influences on willingness to work in later life.

5. Summary and discussion

This chapter explores the life plans and the willingness to work in later life of middle-aged males (40-59). Observations obtained through the analyses performed here can be summarized as follows:

(1) Concerning the life planning of those in their early 60s, only 8.0% said that they intend to live on their pensions/savings. Most people are planning to remain in the workforce in some form.

(2) Regarding the life planning of those in their late 60s, about 70% answered

that they want to remain in the labor market in some form, but only 3.8% said that they will continue to work as "full-time corporate workers." Thus, the employment status they desire will be diversified.

(3) With regard to the life planning of those aged 70 or over, approximately 40% show a willingness to continue to work in some form.

(4) The bigger the economic burden, such as mortgage, they have, the higher the rate of those with a desire to remain in the workforce after the age of 70 becomes.

(5) A higher percentage of people in the cohort of age 55-59, than in the cohort of age 40-44, show a willingness to work after the age of 70.

(6) The later they had the youngest child, the higher their desired retirement age is.

(7) Corporate workers with a stronger desire to become self-employed/start a business tends to be higher in the desired retirement age.

(8) Stronger intention of becoming self-employed/starting business is observed among the corporate workers who are in younger cohorts, have higher educational background and are engaged in sales or professional jobs. In addition, they show more willingness to get involved in social/communal activities other than work.

(9) According to logit analysis concerning willingness to work in later life, the later those in the early 60s had the youngest child, the significantly higher the possibility of taking a job becomes. In the group aged 65 or over, the possibility of taking a job is higher among corporate workers with the intention of becoming self-employed/starting a business.

(10) Multiple regression analysis concerning willingness to work in later life indicates that the later the subjects had the youngest child or the stronger the desire to become self-employed/start a business, the higher the desired retirement age becomes.

From these observations three points can be highlighted concerning the employment of elderly people.

Firstly, those who are now in middle age have a high willingness to work. The relatively young cohort (40-44), than the rest of the middle-aged males surveyed, shows a lower willingness to work after the age of 70. However, most people want to remain in the labor market until 65. In view of this, it can be estimated that Japanese elderly people's willingness to work will remain high in the future.

The second point is the diversification of employment status among those aged 65 or over and with willingness to work. As shown in the analyses of this chapter, about 70% of those aged 65-69 want to take a job, but they prefer flexible working patterns, saying that they will "reduce working hours per day" and "work only a few days a week." In addressing the issue of employment of the aged, consideration should be given to how companies can be flexible in accepting the employees who prefer short-time work.

The third point is that when corporate workers have a desire to become self-employed/start a business, their willingness to work in later life increases. The high employment rate of elderly people in Japan reflects a high ratio of self-employed workers. Recently, however, the number of self-employed workers has been on the decrease. To raise the employment rate of those in later life, it is necessary to promote the switch of employment status from corporate workers to self-employed workers. The analyses in this chapter also show that corporate workers who have the intention of becoming self-employed/starting a business tend to have more willingness to get involved in social (communal) activities. For the self-employed and business owners, it is easier to have an appropriate work-life balance than corporate workers. As a result, willingness to engage in volunteer and other social activities will get higher among the self-employed/business owners than corporate workers. Given these findings, policy support for workers with a desire to become self-employed/start a business will be increasing important in encouraging the elderly to remain in or enter the labor market and promoting volunteer and other social activities.

Notes

[1] The analyses performed in this chapter are based on part of the data (male samples) obtained from a survey concerning the working patterns and life plans of middle aged people, conducted in November 1996 by the Japan Institute for Labour. The survey was conducted of males aged 40-59 and their spouses living within a radius of 50 km from the metropolitan area, encompassing Tokyo, Chiba, Kanagawa and Saitama prefectures. The samples involve 1,700 males and 1,003 females (spouses), who were extracted from the Basic Resident Register by two-stage stratified random sampling. Of the 1,700 male samples, which were used for this chapter, 1,117 (collection rate) were valid. For details, see the Japan Institute for Labour (1998).

[2] The birth cohort here represents the age of the surveyed as of the survey point (1996).

Transition to later life and quality of life[1]

Chapter 4

1. Introduction

For many employees, mandatory retirement can be a crucial transition into later life with serious effects [2]. It can cause discontinuity in one's life, if only temporarily, and can have a large impact on various aspects of daily life, such as one's role in society, available economic resources and social relations. Previous research has shown that the economic and social resources available to retired people, and the socio-cultural context of ageing, are critical determinants of how people cope with mandatory retirement, and to what extent it is possible to make these vital life adjustments. On the other hand, mandatory retirement can also be viewed as an opportunity to pursue a new career in later life, or to discover a new direction in life (Masaoka et al. 1993; Moen 1996)[3].

In Japan, relatively few sociological studies have been conducted on how mandatory retirement affects one's occupational career and working life. In particular, there are few analyses concerning mandatory retirement of female employees, or gender differences following mandatory retirement. In the U.S. several research groups have studied the life courses of full-time female employees, with either professional or managerial careers, from the 1970s, when they entered the workforce, until the moment of retirement (Moen 1996). In contrast, Japanese women have a greater tendency to suspend their careers in order to raise children, or to discontinue working altogether. Therefore, in sociological studies research has mainly focused on life events such as childbearing, child raising, and returning to work and very few studies have been conducted on female employees from middle age to retirement age [4]. It is predicted, however, that the introduction of the Law for Equal Employment Opportunities for Men and Women in Japan will cause an increasing number of women to continue working full-time until the official retirement age. Therefore, in studies concerning implications of mandatory retirement, approaches from a gender perspective may prove necessary [5].

The current study analyzes and explores gender differences in mandatory retirement based on the secondary data currently available, and some suggestions for future research. In particular, we pay attention to the implications of mandatory retirement on the life adjustments of both women and men and the quality of life after retirement. We will concentrate on three critical factors: community resources, bridge jobs, and a work-life habit. The main purposes of the analysis are: 1) to identify occupational career patterns of Japanese men and women after mandatory retirement; 2) to examine gender differences in life adjustments following mandatory retirement; and 3) to determine the relationship between men's work-life habits and their life adjustments after mandatory retirement.

2. Theoretical background

2.1 Mandatory retirement, gender, and community resources

Previous research has shown that long-term relationships with friends, and involvement in the local community, are key factors during the transition to later life. In the U.S., older women have established more and closer social relationships than older men of the same generation (Hatch 1990; Hatch and Bulcroft 1992). In a follow-up study, Moen et al. (1989; 1992) examined the influence of adult community involvement on physical health in later life.

They found that women who participated in any club or organizational activities in their adult years tended to be more positively involved in society and healthier than those who did not. Moen et al. (1989; 1992) attributed their findings to the positive benefits of multiple adult roles: women who have engaged in social activities in adulthood, in addition to the roles of wife and/or mother, have better health in later life (Moen and Dempster-McClain 1989; Moen, Dempster-McClain and Williams 1992).

Depner and Ingersoll (1982) pointed to differences in social network structures between men and women after mandatory retirement. They reported that retired women have more developed support networks and more "inner circles" of very close relationships, than retired men, indicating a gender gap in the formation of personal networks after retirement. Although they did not find a significant difference in social network size between retired women and full-time housewives, they did note a difference with regard to network structure. The support networks of full-time housewives were developed predominantly around relatives, including spouses and children, whereas those of retired women were developed around friends, rather than their children. In addition, retired women were socially more active, such as in public events and club activities. Compared to men and full-time housewives, retired women were the most active in social activities, and had the largest inner circle of friends. The researchers further suggested that having a large inner circle of friends promoted better life adjustments after retirement (Depner and Ingersoll 1982).

Riddick (1982) studied a sample of retired women aged over 65, and found that participation in community activities could enhance one's satisfaction with life after retirement. First, Riddick created a composite variable called the "leisure role" consisting of three factors: friendship interactions, solitary recreational activities, and voluntary association activities. Path analysis demonstrated that the composite variable had most significant influence on satisfaction with life when compared to other variables, such as reemployment, health and income after retirement. Riddick (1982) demonstrated that friendship interactions, and participation in voluntary and other community activities, were more effective for life adjustments of female employees after retirement than reemployment. The aforementioned American studies suggest that, whereas men tend to make life adjustments through reemployment, women are more likely to enhance their QOL through community activities [6].

In Japan, relations between employment in late adulthood (or after mandatory retirement) and participation in the local community have not been researched conclusively. Sugisawa et al. (1997) studied the relationship between retirement in later life and social activities, using "social interactions" and "social activities" as two indicators of social well-being (apart from mental well-being which was measured by the degree of depression). They found that, for men (aged 60), retirement reduced the frequency of social interactions, whereas, for women (also aged 60), retirement increased that frequency. Sugisawa et al. (1997) therefore concluded that women, as compared to men, tended to increase social interactions in areas other than the workplace after retirement (Sugisawa et al. 1997).

Fujisaki (2004) suggested that gender conscious Japanese society allows women to make more easily a "soft landing" after retirement than men. Because women are better than men in developing a community-based social network, women can more easily maintain a sense of continuity in the critical areas of their lives, despite important changes during the transition to later life (Fujisaki 2004). Therefore, in contrast to men, women who have pursued careers, tend to build fundaments for their lives in their local communities, and can enjoy more community resources after retirement.

2.2 Mandatory retirement, bridge jobs, and work-life habits

For women, involvement in the community plays an important role in life adjustment after retirement, whereas, for men, two critical factors are the availability of "bridge jobs", and the degree of commitment to their employment before retirement. In the U.S., Ruhm (1994) found that a considerable number of men find employment in a "bridge job" before leaving the labor force entirely.

Kim and Feldman (2000) have shown that bridge jobs have a large influence on QOL during retirement. In case of early retirement, bridge employment enhances satisfaction with retirement, and life after retirement in general, thus reinforcing the "continuity theory" proposed by Atchley (1989). In short, continued employment makes life adjustments easier for those who retire in later life, suggesting that the continuity of employment after retirement could also help men enhance their life adjustments.

Another important factor before leaving the labor force is the nature and content of occupational careers. When considering life adjustments after retirement, it is necessary to understand that career attainments and habits developed through long-term career jobs can greatly affect life after retirement. Quick and Moen (1998) showed that the higher the autonomy of one's career, the more one feels satisfied with retirement. In Japan, the relationship between companies and their employees is an important factor. Japanese men who commit themselves throughout their life whole-heartedly to corporate society find it difficult to regard mandatory retirement as an opportunity to discover a new direction in life (Amano 1999). One can hypothesize that, in Japan, employees with low occupational autonomy, and who work hard with "company first" in mind, will adapt poorly to life after retirement.

3. Methods

3.1 Data and analysis

The current report makes use of two data sets that are available from surveys conducted by the Research Institute for Senior Life (2002) [7]. The first data set is derived from a sample of retired men and women (aged 55 - 69) from three surveys conducted in 1991, 1996 and 2001 (hereafter called "National Data"), and have many questions in common. It is therefore possible to determine yearly changes in working patterns of older people in the 1990s. Because not all of the questions in the three surveys are the same, there are limitations on the indexes of life adjustments presented in the current paper. To compensate for this, a second data set, composed of research conducted mainly in urban areas in 2003 by the Research Institute for Senior Life (hereafter called "Urban Area Data") is used here as supplementary data.

3.2 Analysis and manipulated variables

The QOL after retirement is analyzed using three indexes: life adjustments, motivation (morale), and satisfaction with life, with particular attention given to the effect of community involvement, careers, and reemployment after retirement. Gender, the year the data was collected, and occupational careers before retirement, are used as independent variables (see Figure 4-1).

Due to intrinsic limitations in the data sets, composite variables were created from the survey questions available, as shown in Table 4-1. In the National Data, the variables used for logistic regression analysis were two factors from among community resources: 1) the "presence or absence of close friends"; and 2) "close relationship with the local community." In order to discern the presence or absence of friends, subjects were asked whether they had sufficient

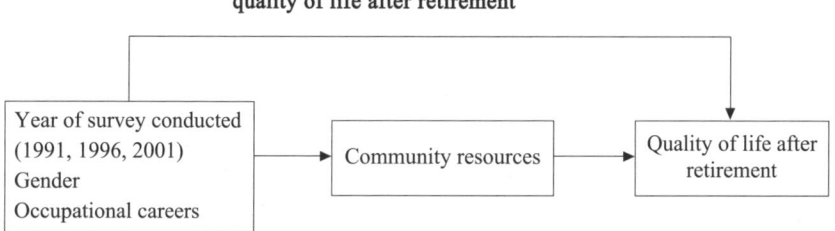

Figure 4-1 Graphical representation of the models explaining quality of life after retirement

```
┌─────────────────────────┐
│ Year of survey conducted│
│ (1991, 1996, 2001)      │──▶ Community resources ──▶ Quality of life after retirement
│ Gender                  │
│ Occupational careers    │
└─────────────────────────┘
```

Table 4-1 Key Statistics of Dependent Variables Used in Analysis

Item	Variable		Mean Value (Standard Deviation (SD))	N
(National Data)				
Community resources	Presence or absence of close friends	(Presence = 1) (Absence = 0)	0.868 (0.339)	2122
	Close relationship with the local community	(high = 1) (low = 0)	0.246 (0.431)	2086
Quality of life	Life adjustment after retirement	(high = 1) (low = 0)	0.707 (0.455)	1547
	Motivation (morale)	(presence = 1) (absence = 0)	0.808 (0.394)	2089
(Urban Area Data)				
Community resources	No. of close friends [1]	(actual number given)	7.312 (8.753)	244
	Amount of social participation [2]	(actual amount in number given)	1.187 (1.267)	257
Quality of life	Satisfaction with life [3]	(rating value given)	28.016 (6.718)	247
	Motivation (morale)	(presence = 1) (absence = 0)	0.717 (0.452)	251

Notes: 1) For the variable of "No. of close friends," actual number of close friends was given.
2) For the variable of "Amount of social participation," the number of groups and organizations people currently belong to was given.
3) For the variable of "Satisfaction with life," 12 questions were posed on a leisurely life and rated on a scale of five, ranging from "very satisfied" to "not satisfied at all."

close friends and companions throughout their lifetimes. Close relationships with the local community and relationships with neighbors were rated on a scale of five by the subjects, ranging from "rarely contact neighbors" to "understand each other's situations and advise or help each other in times of trouble."

In order to assess QOL, two types of variables were used: "life adjustment after retirement" and "presence or absence of motivation (morale)." Life adjustment was calculated based on eight items concerning adaptability to new circumstances after retirement [8]. Here, Cronbach's coefficient alpha, in order to measure life adjustment, was 0.6059. Considering that 1) evaluation of the subject's spouse is included, and 2) there is a significant correlation between "motivation (morale)" and satisfaction with life after retirement, the coefficient alpha is a reliable measure. In logit analysis, life adjustment after retirement was divided into two by the mean value: "1" for above the mean value, and "0" for below [9].

Multiple linear regression analysis was used to analyze the Urban Area Data. Two factors, "number of close friends" and "amount of social participation", were used as the explanatory variables of community resources. Because the Urban Area Data lacks information on close relationships with neighbors, these two factors are used as alternative variables to community resources [10]. Two variables were used to measure QOL: "satisfaction with life" and "presence or absence of motivation." In order to determine "satisfaction with life", subjects were asked a variety of questions regarding leisure life, and rated on a scale of five, ranging from "very satisfied" to "not satisfied at all." In this case, Cronbach's coefficient alpha was 0.8017, which seemed to secure the internal consistency as a measure. The correlation coefficient between "satisfaction with life" and "presence or absence of motivation (morale)" was 0.408, which is significant at a 1% level. Therefore, the two factors of "satisfaction with life" and "motivation (morale)" are used as measures for QOL in the Urban Area Data.

4. Results

4.1 Mandatory retirement and occupational careers

Table 4-2 presents career patterns after retirement by gender based on the National Data set. The rate of employees who left the labor force entirely increased in 2001 as compared to 1991, as indicated by a decrease throughout the decade in employment in old age [11].

Strikingly, there is a significant difference between men and women in the

Table 4-2 Career Patterns after Retirement by Gender [1][2]

		1991	1996	2001
Leaving the workforce entirely	Men	21.1	26.6	30.4
	Women	56.3	61.5	58.4
Working via temporary employment agencies [3]	Men	1.4	2.6	3.4
	Women	1.1	1.3	1.5
Extended employment	Men	31.0	24.9	21.2
	Women	24.1	25.6	27.7
Transferred to subsidiaries	Men	11.8	13.0	16.3
	Women	4.6	2.6	2.2
Reemployment	Men	32.0	28.4	25.7
	Women	10.3	7.7	8.8
Self-employed/running own business [4]	Men	2.8	4.5	3.0
	Women	3.4	1.3	1.5
Total		100.0	100.0	100.0
(N)	Men	(507)	(507)	(565)
	Women	(87)	(78)	(137)
	Total	(594)	(585)	(702)

Notes: 1) The subjects of this study were retirees aged 55 to 69.
2) The figures are based on the National Data.
3) "Working via temporary employment agencies" means employment via temporary employment agencies for senior citizens.
4) "Self-employed/running own business" does not include "helping with the family business."

formation of careers after retirement. More men continued to work after retirement, whereas women were much more likely to leave the labor force completely. As shown in Table 4-2, the ability to extend employment highlights a major gender difference: the percentage of "extended employment" among men decreased from 31.0% to 21.2% between 1991 and 2001, whereas that ability increased among women from 24.1% to 27.7%. This can be attributed to a decline in the number of men whose employment period is extended due to deteriorated employment environment, and concurrently, to an increase in the number of women who have advanced into managerial positions and whose employment is extended.

Table 4-3 shows changes in employment patterns after retirement [12]. During the decade from 1991 to 2001, there was an increase in non-regular employ-

Table 4-3 Changes in Employment Patterns after Retirement [1)2)]

Employment Patterns after Retirement		1991	1996	2001
Regular employment at large companies	Men	5.0	6.5	4.5
	Women	2.6	0.0	4.1
Regular employment at small-to-medium companies	Men	31.5	31.7	28.0
	Women	23.1	25.8	8.2
Non-regular employment at large companies [3)]	Men	18.3	13.7	19.9
	Women	12.8	12.9	20.4
Non-regular employment at small-to-medium companies	Men	38.5	37.4	40.7
	Women	46.2	45.2	51.0
Self-employment [4)]	Men	6.6	10.7	6.9
	Women	15.4	16.1	16.3
Total		100.0	100.0	100.0
(N)	Men	(317)	(262)	(246)
	Women	(39)	(31)	(49)

Notes: 1) The subjects of this study were retirees aged 55 - 69
2) "Non-regular employment" covers dispatched workers, temporary workers and part-time workers.
3) Regarding the size of companies, those with 999 employees or less were categorized as small-to-medium companies, and those with 1000 employees or more as large companies.
4) "Self-employed" includes those helping with the family business.

ment after retirement. The percentage of men working for large companies as non-regular employees grew from 13.7% in 1996 to 19.9% in 2001, and the percentage of those working for small-to-medium businesses also increased from 37.4% to 40.7% during the same period. Similar patterns were seen among women. Between 1996 and 2001 the percentage of non-regular employees among women increased in both large companies (from 12.9% to 20.4%) and small-to-medium companies (from 45.2% to 51.0%). Although this phenomenon is common to both genders, women in particular have enjoyed a rapid increase in non-regular employment in small-to-medium businesses. The percentage of women who are working at small-to-medium sized companies exceeded 50% of the total employment in 2001.

The career patterns after retirement can be summarized as follows: men tend to remain in the labor force after retirement, whereas women tend to leave the labor market entirely or remain there as non-regular employees. The

National Data demonstrate that gender differences exist in career formations after retirement.

4.2 Gender differences in the process of mandatory retirement

The National Data were analyzed for gender differences in career formation using logistic regression analysis, with QOL after retirement as the dependent variable (Table 4-4).

Women tended to have more lifelong friends ($\beta = 0.863$) and to establish closer relationships with the local community than men ($\beta = 0.425$). Conversely, men were less involved in communities than women. Persons who had been more involved in communities tended to have more motivation after retirement ($\beta = 1.266$), and there was more motivation among those who re-entered the workforce after retirement than those who did not ($\beta = 0.349$). The data indicated that QOL was enhanced by involvement in communities, or by re-entering the labor market, after retirement. The results of the logit analysis showed that, although there was no difference between men and women in life adjustments after retirement, there could be a gender difference in the process of life adjustments after retirement.

As depicted in Table 4-2, men were more likely than women to re-enter the labor force after retirement. Table 4-4 indicates that reemployment after retirement has a positive effect on motivation. For men, continuing work after retirement enhanced motivation, whereas women tended to leave the labor market entirely when reaching retirement age, or to work as non-regular employees, when they decided to remain in the workforce after retirement. It is highly possible that women maintained their motivation by possessing various social resources, such as closer relationships with friends and the local community.

Table 4-4 Logistic Regression Analysis concerning Life Adjustment after Retirement[1]

	"Community Resources" Index		"Quality of Life" Index	
	Presence or absence of close friends	Close relationship with the local community	Life Adjustment	Motivation (Morale)
	β (exp)	β (exp)	β (exp)	β (exp)
Sex (vs. Men)				
Women	.863**(2.369)	.425**(1.529)	−.014 (.986)	.152 (.859)
Year of survey (vs.1991)				
1996	−.083 (.921)	−.042 (.959)	.110 (1.116)	.867***(2.381)
2001	.075 (1.077)	.245+ (1.278)	.041 (1.042)	.253 (1.264)
Careers after retirement (vs.reemployment)[2]				
Leaving the workforce entirely	−.249 (.779)	−.380* (.684)	.553** (1.738)	−.182 (.833)
Extended employment	−.390* (.677)	−.446** (.640)	.457* (1.580)	−.189 (.828)
Transferred to subsidiaries	−.085 (.918)	−.369+ (.692)	.320 (1.377)	−.330 (.719)
Self-employed/running own business[3]	.352 (1.422)	.273 (1.314)	−.121 (.886)	.657 (1.929)
Employment after retirement (presence)	−.254 (.775)	−.246+ (.782)	.610***(1.841)	.349* (1.418)
Academic background (vs. high school graduates or lower education)				
Junior college/vocational school graduate	.440 (1.553)	−.034 (.966)	−.082 (.921)	.216 (1.241)
College graduate or higher education	.296+ (1.345)	−.933***(.393)	.041 (1.042)	−.045 (.956)
Health (good)	.166+ (1.181)	.282***(1.325)	.197***(1.218)	.410***(1.506)
Close friends (presence)			.092 (1.097)	1.266***(3.547)
Close relationship with the local community (high)			.286+ (1.331)	.512** (1.669)
Constant	.495 (1.641)	−2.208***(.110)	−.577 (.561)	−1.395***(.248)
−2 Log Likelihood	1293.112	1700.136	1435.569	1455.257
Model Chi-Square	29.094**	79.149***	33.841**	152.372***
N	1664	1638	1225	1608

Significance level: *** <.001 ** <.01 * <.05 + .10

Notes: 1) For the analysis, retired men and women aged 55-69 were used as a sample.
2) Those working via temporary employment agencies and their figures were not included in the sample.
3) "Self-employed" includes those helping with the family business.

Table 4-5 Factor Structure of Occupational Autonomy [1)2)]

	Company-Harmonized autonomy	Independence-oriented autonomy
Engaged in activities outside the company	**.800**	.064
Made efforts to improve occupational abilities on an individual basis	**.717**	.308
Lifelong employment was a pillar for life planning	**.617**	−.503
Active at social interactions outside the company	.109	**.558**
Did nothing special except for work	.033	**−.622**
Prepared for job transfer/becoming independent	.027	**.598**
Eigen value	1.55	1.41
Variance (%)	25.8	23.5
No. of samples	242	

Notes: 1 The figures in the upper block of the table show factor loadings obtained from a principal component analysis using varimax rotation.
2 From the Urban Area Data, retired men aged 55-69 were used as a sample for analysis.

4.3 Men's occupational attitude and life adjustments

The relationship between occupational attitude and QOL after retirement among men was analyzed using the Urban Area Data. Table 4-5 presents the factor analysis of the degree of personal commitment to a company as a work-life habit [13].

Two types of occupational autonomy were created: "company-harmonized autonomy" and "independence-oriented autonomy." People with company-harmonized autonomy made efforts to enhance their work ability within the context of the lifetime employment system, and were also involved in activities outside the company. These employees placed great importance on enhancing the autonomy of work through adjustment and adaptation to the corporate environment, rather than by leaving the corporate organization. This form of autonomy is not contradictory to life planning based on lifelong employment. In short, the autonomy of work can coexist with lifelong employment. In contrast, people with independence-oriented autonomy were very proactive in preparing for a career switch, possibly by starting their own businesses while actively interacting with individuals outside the company. Employees with independ-

Table 4-6 Multiple Linear Regression Analysis concerning Life Adjustments after Retirement

	"Community Resources" Index		"Quality of Life" Index	
	No. of close friends	Amount of social participation	Satisfaction with life	Motivation (morale)
Age	−.021	.048	.053	.093
Academic background	.245***	.110+	−.011	.049
Health	.094	.170*	.441***	.232**
Employment after retirement	−.025	.024	−.014	.052
Company-harmonized autonomy	.203**	.178**	.149*	.172**
Independence-oriented autonomy	.058	.015	−.031	−.050
R^2	.120	.085	.222	.108
F value	4.623***	3.341**	9.960***	4.261***
N	210	223	217	218

Note: Significance level *** < .001 ** < .01 * < .05 + .10

ence-oriented autonomy tended to have stronger aspirations of independence from corporate organizations without relying on lifelong employment.

Table 4-6 depicts the relationship among occupational autonomy, community resources and QOL after retirement. Multiple linear regression analysis showed that company-harmonized autonomy had a significant effect on "number of friends" (β = 0.203), on "amount of social participation" (β = 0.178), on "satisfaction with life" (β = 0.149) and on "motivation" (β = 0.172), the latter two serving here as indexes of QOL.

In contrast, independence-oriented autonomy did not show any significant effect on those variables. Male employees demonstrated that harmony with their companies, rather than independence from corporate organizations, helped them to improve their QOL after retirement.

5. Conclusions and discussion

The aim of the current chapter was to identify possible relationships between occupational careers and QOL of men and women after retirement. Although both genders demonstrated high indexes of life adjustments and motivation, they differed in their involvement in communities after retirement. Women were more likely to have a wider network of friends and to interact more closely with neighbors than men. Such involvement in communities had a positive effect on life adjustments after retirement. Similarly, in case of men, continuing to work after retirement also had a positive effect on life adjustments. These so-called bridge jobs were effective in improving QOL in later life after retirement. Men, who were more likely than women to continue work after retirement, tended to make life adjustments via reemployment. In contrast, women, who were more inclined than men to leave the labor market, or be engaged in non-regular employment, made life adjustments via community resources, including inner-circles of lifelong friends and neighbors [14].

How can gender differences in mandatory retirement be explained from a sociological viewpoint? First, mandatory retirement can be examined in terms of "continuity" in a course of life (Fujisaki 2004). Fujisaki claimed that, in Japan, men maintained their motivation through the continuity of careers, by remaining in the labor market after retirement, whereas women maintained continuity via relationships with friends and the local community, rather than via new careers. Second, mandatory retirement can be examined in terms of plurality of life worlds. Persons represented in the current chapter were full-time employees who worked until mandatory retirement. Female employees were often also wives and/or mothers, and were yet able to maintain close relationships with communities other than family members. These findings collaborate the results of Moen (1992), in which the plurality of life worlds had a positive effect on adjustments in later life.

Many Japanese men work long hours every day as "company-first" employees, and thus may be less committed to family roles such as husbands and fathers. Working women, however, often have no other choice than to perform multiple roles, as they continue to raise children and perform household duties. It is these differences between men and women in the flexibility of attitudes toward work and plurality of life worlds that likely have a major influence on life adjustments after mandatory retirement. Men, with one-dimensional roles as company-first employees tend to maintain continuity by remaining in the workforce after retirement, whereas women, who fill multiple roles everyday, can make life adjustments relatively smoothly during mandatory retirement. As Imada (1991) stated, women view mandatory retirement as a "challenge to deal with in life, and a product of coordination." The plurality of life worlds observed among retired women, can provide the answer for developing happy lives for men after retirement. This plurality can be created, not only by having commitment to work, but also by establishing a network of friends and securing roles to play in a status-oriented society while adjusting the balance in everyday life.

This chapter also analyzed the "company-harmonized autonomy" in occupational attitude of men before retirement, and demonstrated via factor analysis that male work-life habits had a strong positive effect on life adjustments after retirement. In the U.S., occupational autonomy has been shown to have a positive effect on satisfaction with retirement, whereas, in Japan occupational autonomy linked to 'harmony with the corporate organization' had a more positive influence. Recent research conducted in Japanese companies has found that, since the latter half of the 1970s, there has been an increase in the number of corporate employees who are not full-time engaged in work (Sato 1999). Thus, a growing number of corporate employees, including white-collar workers of large companies, have kept themselves at arm's length from the company and desire to expand their activities into other realms. This does not imply, however, that aspirations to work for a company have not declined. Although a growing number of Japanese corporate employees wanted to become involved in the company in a limited way, there has not been a drop in expectations for lifelong employment. This tendency coincides with "company-harmonized autonomy," which was observed among the retired male employees analyzed in this chapter. An occupational attitude, established during many years of working life, also determined how one lives after retirement. In Japan, life adjustments after retirement are easier to make if one's work-life habit put weight on company-harmonized autonomy, supported by lifelong employment, rather than an occupational attitude with emphasis on job switching or becoming self-employed. In this respect, the current research findings differ from those found in the U.S., where the job market is mature and provides a favorable environment for switching their jobs. In Japan, harmony with the company type of attitudes play a more important role in later life careers and life adjustments, whereas, in the U.S., individualistic and independence-oriented autonomy may be more effective.

Lastly, the present studied the effect of mandatory retirement from the perspective of the life course. One of the advantages of this approach is that it gives sufficient attention to longitudinal changes by using a cohort comparison study. Moen (1996) stated that gender differences in life adjustments after retirement can be explained by considering the changing times in the U.S. A review of empirical data collected in the 1970s in the U.S., when female employment rate was low, showed that women were generally more satisfied with retirement than men, or that women were more likely than men to make a positive assessment concerning retirement (Moen 1996). At a time when careers were less often interrupted by life events, such as childbearing and child rearing, and when there was less awareness of the role of female employees, women tended to show higher satisfaction with retirement. Data collected since the 1980s, however, indicate that women in the U.S. now feel less satisfied with retirement than men. Thus, emancipation movements in the 1980s and full-scale female employment in the 1990s significantly changed the meaning of retirement as compared to working women in the 1970s (Quick and Moen 1998). Social cohorts, with different social climates and various historical backgrounds, possess different meanings of, and attitudes toward, retirement. Further comparative research needs to be conducted in order to investigate the life courses of women whose status has radically changed in the labor market, and specifically gender-related differences concerning mandatory retirement.

Notes:

[1] This paper was originally submitted in Japanese to Ritsumeikan Social Sciences Review, 2005 (Vol. 41, No. 1), and has been subsequently translated into English.

[2] Mandatory retirement in Japan has a different meaning from retirement in Western countries. In Japan, many older people who face mandatory retirement continue to work in some form, whereas, in Western countries, retirement denotes that people finish their careers. In Japan, mandatory retirement implies that people reach a crucial turning point in their lives, where they should develop other careers in later life (see Maeda, 2003).

[3] Japan's retirement system is a mandatory retirement scheme based on age, which was introduced into major companies in the early Showa era (1926-1989). It has become common practice since the end of World War II (Inagami 1993).

[4] Pioneering research concerning mandatory retirement (Aoi and Wada 1983) used male subjects exclusively, and therefore, the working lives of middle-aged or older women remains unclear.

[5] Even in the U.S., it is said that sociological studies neglected the retirement of women until the 1980s (Szinovacz 1982).

[6] Recent sociological analysis concerning mandatory retirement indicated men with jobs tended to show higher morale than those without jobs, when the variable of personal health condition was corrected for (Naoi 2001). On the other hand, women did not show any significant relationship between the presence or absence of a job, and morale (Naoi 2001).

[7] In this chapter, data was collected from retirees of companies that have entered the Employees' Pension Scheme, and the samples were drawn from corporate employees who worked until the official retirement age. Self-employed workers were not included in the samples. To enter the Employees' Pension Scheme, all employees (including part-time workers) are required to work more than three-fourths of the working hours of regular employees (more than 30 hours per week). Hence, the samples used in the present paper can be regarded as regular, full-time employees. For this reason, the rate of those starting their own businesses after retirement is lower than that of national standard samples. Here, focus was put on the process of mandatory retirement of men and women who were regular full-

time employees.

⁸ Subjects were asked whether they experienced any of the following life events from the start of retirement until the present moment (where applicable, "-1" was added). Note that, because data was collected on both retirees and their spouses, the number of entries doubled:
- My relationships with family members have deteriorated;
- I have lost morale or motivation in life;
- I feel lonely because of the loss of title/a sense of belonging;
- I feel inconvenience because of a decrease in social interactions and the volume of information;
- I am at a loss because I cannot catch up with the advancement of the information-oriented society;
- I have a strong sense of being isolated from society;
- I have too much time on hand; and
- I find it difficult to integrate into the local community.

⁹ The variables of "life adjustments after retirement" in the National Data include the assessment of the subjects themselves and that of their spouses. Those without a spouse were removed from the samples; therefore the number of samples is fewer than other variables used in the analysis.

¹⁰ Kaneko (1993) analyzed the community network of elderly people by examining "close relations with neighbors"

¹¹ Changes in employment rate after retirement have been largely affected by legal restrictions in the retirement system. In 1994, the Law Concerning Stabilization of Employment of Older Persons was revised, requiring companies to make the retirement of employees compulsory at the age of 60. This law was then enforced in 1998. Three data sets were analyzed in the current report: data sets from 1991 and 1996 were compiled when retirement of employees at the age of 60 was not mandatory, but was up to the discretion of employers. The data indicated that the retirement rate among people under 60 was high. The data set generated in 2001 showed that the retirement age was roughly 60 or over. As a result, the reemployment rate after retirement was lower in 2001 than in 1991. This result corresponds to the National Data compiled from surveys conducted by the central government (The Association of Employment Development for Senior Citizens, 2003). Refer to Nishimura (2004) for regulations concerning the mandatory retirement system.

¹² In Table 4-3, "self-employed" includes "helps with the family business." These two items were considered less than one heading because they could not be separated from one another for the reason of experimental design. As a result, many women belong to the item

"self-employed," of which many are family employees.

[13] Refer to Ikeda (2003) for further explanations of "occupational autonomy," "work-life habit" and manipulated variables.

[14] Non-regular employment can be viewed as one form of employment from the viewpoints of health and life adjustments. Refer to Maeda (2000) and Maeda (2002) for the relationships between "typical employment" and life, and between the male way of working and family life, respectively.

Social Networks in Later Life

Chapter 5

1. Social isolation of the elderly

The "lonely senior" is a common image we have of elderly people. The image that elderly people are lonely stems partly from public concern over a reduced social network or isolation from society through poor interpersonal relationships within families, the workplace and the local community in later life. In 1993, for example, the Prime Minister's Office conducted a poll concerning the image of life in later life. The highest proportion of the respondents (39.7%) view life in later life as a "life with anxiety in economic, health and other aspects," which is almost equivalent to the rate of the respondents (38.9%) saying that it is "a life of leisure after retiring from the front line." As much as 14.7% see their later stage of life as being a lonely existence with poor relationships with family and those around them, exceeding the responses of "a fulfilling life as the golden age of life" (12.2%) and "a life free from constraints" (11.9%). Indeed, social environment surrounding elderly people undergoes a more significant change than in the young and middle-aged. Men, in particular, are more likely to be isolated from society since retirement brings about a poor relationship with the workplace. (McCallum, 1987)

However, the negative image of loneliness in later life might be due to the gap between the rapidly changing social environment surrounding elderly people and current public awareness of ageing. An example is a recent change in family structure. A glance at changes in the family structure of elderly people shows that a declining number of senior citizens are living their life under the same roof as their children and grandchildren. In contrast, there has been an increase in the percentage of single-person and husband-wife households.[1] At the same time, it should be noted that a decreasing number of people believe that family members should be obligated to take care of elderly parents. The stem family system, under which elder parents are taken care of by their sons or daughters under the same roof, is no longer taken for granted.[2] When their spouses stay fit and well, elderly people can live by themselves. In some situations, however, they have no other choice but to live alone. The problem is that despite drastic changes in family structure, people still tend to have a positive image of three generations living together under one roof, thereby making it hard to recognize the current existing image of social relationships that has replaced the traditional pattern.

Considering the historical transformation of the family system in Europe and the United States, it can be assumed that Japan will also see a rapid decline in the rate of three generations living under one roof. In a society where the idea that personal independence becomes the nucleus of the social relationships of the elderly has yet to be widely accepted, a declining number of three generations living under the same roof and a weakened sense of responsibility for supporting elderly parents may be driving people to have the negative image of elderly people being isolated and suffering social-related anxiety.

However, is it true that elderly people have become isolated due to the collapse of Japan's traditional family system? If so, measures should be taken to tackle this social issue. If the theory is wrong, however, it is necessary to clarify what relationships elderly people have built up within society. Clarifying the realities of the social environment surrounding elderly people will help to understand how to provide the elderly with institutional/policy support that allows them to live on their own while maintaining better relationships with society. This chapter explores elderly people's relationships with society by using a sociological methodology with a focus on "social networks."

2. Concept of social networks

Before exploring the social relationships of the elderly, the concept of social networks should be referred to. In sociology, the conventional approach is to analyze social relationships, using reference groups. Such groups include a workplace group, a community group, and a family. Since these groups are assumed to be a system with a specific boundary, analysis is often made with the focus on their structure and function (Boissevain, 1974). However, when emphasis is laid on the development of individuals, the perspective that a particular individual selects his own social relationships as a resource under a given social environment comes to the fore. Each individual belongs to a certain group with such a clear boundary or function. At the same time, they often selectively develop a relationship with several social units. Given this perspective, it is important to create a theoretical framework to analyze the links between social units by regarding each individual as a starting point, rather than analyzing the structure or function of each group. These social relation-

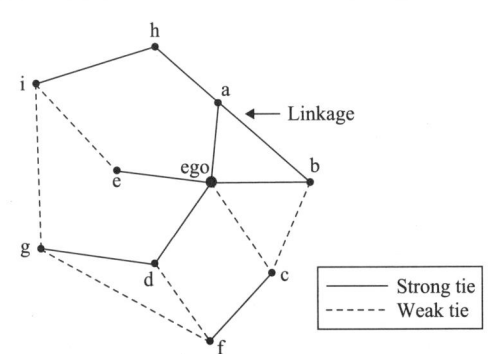

Figure 5-1 Seniors' Social Networks and Linkage

ships selectively developed by a particular person are called "social networks." The "social network" approach puts stress on each individual as a subjective unit rather than analyzing the structure or functions of each group. Social networks mean the relationships that people develop with others during their life course, which can be regarded as a resource from a sociological perspective (Meguro, 1988).

There are existing concepts of social networks. The most fundamental notion is a linkage, which shows how connections are built up to form a network.[3] As shown in Figure 5-1, "ego," or an individual, connects to other units by means of linkages, and there are no limits to the expansion of this network. Those linkages vary in strength, ranging from what could be regarded as a strong tie to a weak tie. The connecting units can be either a group or an individual. When an analysis is conducted of a family or community, however, ego (individual) is often regarded as the center of the network. The connection in social networks can be described by using other various concepts, such as size, density, centrality, tie strength, and range (Hall and Wellman, 1985; Marsden, 1987, 1990).

The use of such concepts to describe social networks allows quantitative determination of family relationships, not through the conventionally dichotomous approach in which families are divided into two - a nuclear family or stem family. Traditional families, especially in Japan, can be divided merely into two types: a nuclear family and a stem family. A map of a transition from a stem family to a nuclear family is based on the dichotomous typology. When the concepts conventionally used in family sociology are replaced with the social network concepts, however, the social network theory suggests how to reconsider the dichotomous typology. For instance, a stem family generally means that a husband, his elderly parent(s), wife and children live under the same roof (live on the same site). When this type of family is measured by means of various notions of social networks, such as frequency, density and size, it reveals that its contents vary. In some nuclear families, even though not living on the same site, a husband and wife may contact their parents living far away more frequently and have more communication with them, than those within a stem family. From a social network perspective, some nuclear families have relationships with elderly parents that are equal to or closer than stem families. In other words, families used to be grouped based on the notion of spatial distance and divided into two types: living under the same roof or not. In theory at least, however, it is possible to redefine family as part of the social networks, in terms of frequency, density, size as well as spatial distance.

Some elderly people who live alone may have closer relationships with their families and relatives than those living as a member of a stem family. For determining the subjective social relationships of elderly people, it is more appropriate to use the social network concepts to measure the relationships with family, which is a resource for elderly people, in both quantitative and qualitative terms.

Another advantage of using the social network concepts is to allow us to understand how extensively elderly people develop social relationships, not merely to conduct an analysis with focus on family and kin. Given that there will be an increase in the number of elderly people living on their own in the future, it is more important to conduct analyses with a focus on new social relationships, including neighbors, friends, and professional services, rather than to place importance on whether the elderly are living with their families or not (Wellman et al., 1988).

In social network studies in Western countries, attempts have been made to classify the social networks that elderly people have with their families, relatives, neighbors and friends, according to type (Wenger, 1992, 1994). In Japan as well, it will be a challenge to redefine the types of elderly people's relationships with their families and communities by applying a methodology and quantitatively determining the scope of social networks in terms of frequency, density and size. In such cases, how to discriminate between families and neighbors/friends depends on the basic measures used. However, it is possible to reexamine the conventional patterns of families and communities. It will also become an extremely useful notion in considering how families are selected as part of social networks, with an individual as the point of origin. The application of the social network notions will allow the fact to emerge that a family is a resource through which to satisfy the needs of each individual and is chosen as one of his/her social networks.

3. Studies on the social networks of Japanese elderly

The notions of social networks have been widely applied to studies in the fields of urban sociology, family sociology and other organizational studies.[4] There are some experimental studies concerning the social networks of elderly people. Among them, Isamu Kaneko (1987) has approached squarely the issue of isolation among elderly people from the perspective of social networks. His analyses were made of seniors' social networks with the focus on their relationships with neighbors. The main purpose of his analyses was to verify the general image of ageing and loneliness. The two basic items for study used in his analyses were 'locality-relevant network' and 'non-locality-relevant network.' As part of the study, Kaneko undertook a survey concerning the social networks of elderly people living in the two Japanese cities of Otaru and Kurume. The result showed the existence of highly developed networks, in both qualitative and quantitative terms, observed in the two cities. Concerning the non-locality-relevant network in particular, there was a very strong mutual exchange between elderly people and their adult children who lived elsewhere. For elderly people, a close correlation is also found between a life satisfaction and a relationship with the local community. These findings indicate that the elderly in general are by no means isolated from society, and if anything, they tend to make the best use of the network of kinship, local communities, and friends. Kaneko concluded that it is necessary to modify the general image of elderly people being lonely (Kaneko, 1987:341).

On the other hand, Nobuhiko Maeda experimentally revealed what types of social networks elderly people form based on qualitative studies, and also examined the issue of isolated senior citizens. Maeda's key theme was to identify whether the "community liberated" argument in Western urban sociology, especially based on Barry Wellman's work (Wellman, 1979), can be applied to the community of senior citizens in Japan, which is discussed in chapter 6 of this book. To substantiate the theory, he applied the three models of "community lost," "community saved," and "community liberated" to the community of elderly people living in urban areas in Japan. As a result, it was discovered that senior citizens in urban areas have established a broader social network of distant friends and they are neither isolated nor confined to traditional community ties. In other words, Japanese seniors living in urban areas have developed a broader social network of friends, transcending the framework of a local community, while keeping close contact with their adult children living elsewhere and people in the neighborhood. This falls into the "community liberated" model. Generally, Japanese elderly people have established rich social networks in quantitative and qualitative terms, exhibiting expanded and diversified social networks.

Thus, the phenomenon of seniors isolated from their families/kin was not observed despite the recent drastic change in the family system. In reality, many have developed new social relationships depending on the situations they are placed in. As far as earlier studies are concerned, therefore, it cannot be said that elderly people in Japan are isolated, as mentioned at the beginning of this chapter. From the viewpoint of experimental studies, it seems necessary to alter the general image that elderly people are lonely. Next, the structure of social networks developed by the elderly is discussed, with the issue of isolated seniors in mind.

4. Social network structure of the elderly

Firstly, the personal community of the elderly should be examined by four measures: size of personal community, geographical distance, the frequency of interaction, and the length of relationship.

Table 5-1 provides the size of elderly people's networks with children living elsewhere, relatives, neighbors and friends. As shown on the far right of the table, the average of the size of each network is highest in friends (4.61), followed by neighbors (3.39), relatives (2.98) and children living elsewhere (1.62). As far as the size of social networks is concerned, the personal community of elderly people is established centering on their friends. It can be repre-

Table 5-1 Seniors' Social Networks: Size (%)

	0	1	2	3	4	5	6+	Average (variance)
Children living elsewhere	22.4	25.8	30.3	13.9	5.4	1.5	0.7	1.62 (1.28)
Relatives	23.5	16.4	14.8	13.7	6.8	9.6	15.3	2.98 (3.41)
Neighbors	37.9	8.2	8.4	12.6	5.4	10.7	16.8	3.39 (6.25)
Friends	34.4	6.7	8.4	12.4	5.1	10.2	22.9	4.61 (9.42)

Note: Figures in the far right column represent the average and variance of the size of each network (no. of people).

Table 5-2 Seniors' Social Networks: Geographical Distance (time required) (%)

	Less than 10 min.	10 to 30 min.	30 min. to 1 hr.	1 hr. to 2 hrs.	2 hrs. or more	Average [1] (variance)
Children living elsewhere	23.2	17.9	25.5	19.4	14.1	2.83 (1.36)
Relatives	15.0	14.3	27.5	21.8	21.3	3.20 (1.33)
Neighbors [2]	–	–	–	–	–	– (–)
Friends	17.4	26.5	29.3	17.5	9.3	2.75 (1.20)

Notes: 1) Figures in the far right column represent average geographical distance in each network type; the larger the figure is, the longer the geographical distance.
2) Geographical distance was not measured for seniors' social networks with neighbors.

sented as friends > neighbors > relatives > children living elsewhere. In this respect, what is important is that the size of seniors' networks with neighbors exceeds that of their networks with kin. It is often said that Japan's traditional local community system collapsed with the rapid progress of industrialization and urbanization. However, this survey has found that elderly people have developed a more solid network with neighbors than expected, not the type of networks resulting from the collapse of local community ties.

Table 5-2 shows the geographical distance of social networks by measuring how much time it takes elderly people to access their children living elsewhere, relatives, and friends. The figures (average) on the far right of the table mean that the larger the figure is, the further the geographical distance (required time). Relatives are living furthest away (3.20), followed by children living elsewhere (2.83), and friends (2.75). In this case, neighbors were not included since they are obviously in the neighborhood. In decreasing order, the geographical distance of social networks can be expressed as: relatives > children living elsewhere > friends > neighbors. Thus, neighbors are the core of seniors' personal community structure, around which there are friends and children living elsewhere, and the most exterior is kin.

Table 5-3 provides the frequency of interaction by the type of social networks. The figures (average) on the far right of the table mean that the larger the figure is, the higher the frequency of interaction. Frequency of interaction

Table 5-3 Seniors' Social Networks: Frequency of Interaction (%)

	Nearly every day	Once a week or more	Once a month or more	2-3 times a year	Once a year or less	Average (variance)
Children living elsewhere	18.0	17.4	39.4	22.2	3.0	4.97 (1.95)
Relatives	8.0	7.2	27.4	39.3	18.2	3.79 (1.80)
Neighbors	31.9	47.2	18.3	2.4	0.2	6.60 (1.38)
Friends	4.3	24.4	32.0	26.1	13.2	4.32 (1.78)

Note: Figures in the far right column represent average frequency of interaction; the larger the figure is, the higher the frequency of interaction.

is measured by the question "How often do you meet with Mr.(Ms.)X?" According to the table, neighbors (6.60) are highest in the frequency of interaction, followed by children living elsewhere (4.97), friends (4.32) and relatives (3.79). What is worth noting here is that nearly 80% of the elderly people surveyed see their neighbors "almost every day" or "once a week or more," presenting higher contact frequency than other network groups. The contact frequency can be expressed in decreasing order as: neighbors > children living elsewhere > friends > relatives. The average contact frequency is very close between children living elsewhere and friends. However, variance shows that 13.2% of those surveyed see their friends "once a year or less" while 18.0% see their children living elsewhere "nearly every day." Given this situation, the frequency of interaction with children living elsewhere should be considered higher than friends. As with the analysis of the size of social networks, the contact frequency per network type also indicates the superiority of neighborhood ties. The frequency of contact with siblings and other relatives is lowest, revealing that elderly people are more remotely related to their kin than their children living elsewhere.

Table 5-4 provides the length of relationship per network type. In this case, measurement was not made for children living elsewhere and relatives. Figures on the far right represent average length of relationship; the larger the figure is, the longer the relationship. It is found that the elderly people surveyed have

Table 5-4 Seniors' Social Networks: Length of Relationship (%)

	Less than 10 yrs.	10 to 20 yrs.	20 to 30 yrs.	30 to 40 yrs.	40 yrs or more	Average [1] (variance)
Children living elsewhere [2]	–	–	–	–	–	– (–)
Relatives	–	–	–	–	–	– (–)
Neighbors	15.6	19.3	21.6	20.5	23.0	25.0 (16.2)
Friends	12.6	17.5	20.5	17.2	32.2	28.4 (17.5)

Notes: 1) Figures in the far right column represent average length of relationship (no. of years); the larger the figure is, the longer the relationship.
2) The length of relationship with children living elsewhere and relatives was not measured.

more than 20 years of relationships with neighbors and friends. The point worth noting here is that 23% and 32.2% of the subjects had more than 40 years, which is more than half of their life span, of relationships with neighbors and friends, respectively.

Thus, the analysis by the four measures of network size, geographical distance, contact frequency, and the length of relationship has disclosed two major characteristics of seniors' personal community.

Firstly, the personal community of elderly people is formed centering on friends. The comparison of the size of networks indicates that a network of friends is largest, followed by neighbors and relatives. It is worthy of note that elderly people have nearly 5 friends on average. The distribution maps of geographical distance and the frequency of interaction show that elderly people have a closer relationship with their neighbors than their kin. This analysis does not disclose how much support elderly people give to or receive from their friends. Judging from network size, geographical distance, contact frequency and the length of relationship, however, it can be considered that friends, rather than siblings and other relatives, serve a more important support function.

The second characteristic is the superiority of the "neighborhood" network in the personal community of elderly people. The analysis made in this chapter has found that the size of a neighborhood network is larger than a network of kin; a vast majority interact with neighbors once a week or more, and there is a long relationship with neighbors. In terms of geographical distance, it is found that elderly people have a closer relationship with neighbors than friends in everyday life. As mentioned earlier, it is often said that in Japan where rapid urbanization and significant population shifts have occurred, a traditional local community system has collapsed with the advent of the high economic growth era. This survey targeting elderly people, however, disclosed the superiority of neighborhood relationships in a personal community. Since seniors cannot travel around as easily as young and middle-aged people, they tend to create an everyday life by building a broader relationship with the neighborhood. However, given that elderly people have a closer relationship with their friends than relatives and also maintain contact with distant friends, it can be considered that they have established a personal community in which a network of friends and relatives are used selectively, while keeping networks with neighbors and children living elsewhere as the basis of their personal community, rather than living in a traditional close-knit community. Fig. 5-2 provides the spatial distribution of the personal community of elderly people living in urban areas.

As shown in the oval model, neighbors live closest to and interact most frequently with "ego." Friends and children living elsewhere are positioned in the outer region of neighbors, and relatives (siblings), to whom the ego is relatively remotely related, are in the outermost oval.

As far as the findings of this chapter are concerned, different types of social

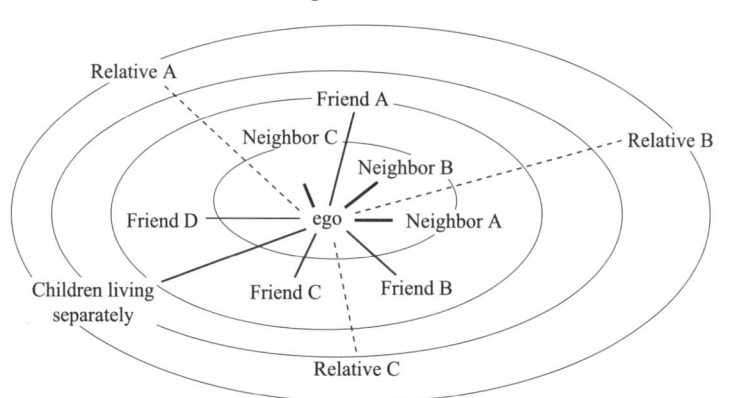

Figure 5-2 Spatial Distribution of Personal Community: Senior Citizens Living in Urban Areas

Note: The further network members are situated from the ego, the longer geographical distance is. The ranking of frequency of interaction, from highest to lowest, is a bold solid line, a solid line and dotted line. This distribution map is based on the average values of seniors' social network size, geographical distance and frequency of interaction.

networks show differences in geographical distances and the frequency of interaction in modern Japan's urban society. In other words, it can be considered that elderly people have formed a ramified network that is expected in any liberated model of personal community. Urbanization does not drive elderly people into isolation from society, but encourages them to selectively utilize a network of friends or relatives, while keeping close ties with neighbors and children living nearby. Maeda (1993) also undertook a study on the social networks of middle-aged women living in urban areas to verify the theory of personal community. The same findings were obtained in that study, except for the development of the neighborhood network. This difference can be attributable to a difference in the samples used; most data used in this chapter is from those living in *Shitamachi*, or the old downtown area of Tokyo. Another reason is that during the process of ageing from middle age to advanced age, there might be the development of a network with neighbors, resulting from their decreased mobility. It is hard to comprehend how social networks have changed through time, since the two studies do not share the same samples. However, it can be assumed that the ageing of people helps enhance the importance of a neighborhood network.

5. Typology of social network

In this section, the focus is on the social network structure of senior citizens, using recently acquired data.[5] Based on community studies conducted by Canadian sociologist Barry Wellman, seniors' social networks are divided into three. The first is the "isolated" type of social networks, in which senior citizens are isolated without developing social networks. The second is the "traditional" type of social networks, or social networks limited to a local community, in which elderly people have abundant social networks, but their networks are confined to a specific area, such as participation in neighborhood associations, local clubs and other local community activities. The last is the "liberated" type of social networks, which corresponds with Wellman's liberated argument. Those classified in this type develop a broader social network of friends, while establishing a close relationship with their children living elsewhere and neighbors as the basis of their social networks. In this case, it is expected that elderly people tend to keep in touch with friends living far away as well as those nearby.

Given that the objective of this chapter is to examine the issue of seniors isolated from society, first, attention should be paid to the presence of isolated elderly people. One objective of the analysis is to identify how many isolated citizens there are. Secondly, a liberated type of social networks is discussed. As indicated by Wellman, this is a new type of urban community based on social networks. It means that elderly people have a new social relationship through a broader friend-based network beyond the scope of a local community while keeping close ties with their families and neighbors as the basis of their social networks, rather than participation in local community activities/units through closely-knit ties with those in the neighborhood, which are often observed in traditional communities.

Here, the types of social networks are defined according to the size of a network (no. of people). An extremely small social network is regarded as "isolated." When people have a large size of network but are highly involved in a local community, the network is viewed as "traditional/local community-oriented." And a broad friend-based network is seen as "liberated."[6] Details of

Table 5-5 Seniors' Social Networks: Size
(persons)

	Children living elsewhere	Neighbors	Extended relatives	Friends	Total
Isolated type	1.60	0.48	0.68	0.39	3.14
Traditional type	1.53	4.98	4.63	3.48	14.63
Liberated type	1.51	3.49	2.91	6.88	14.79

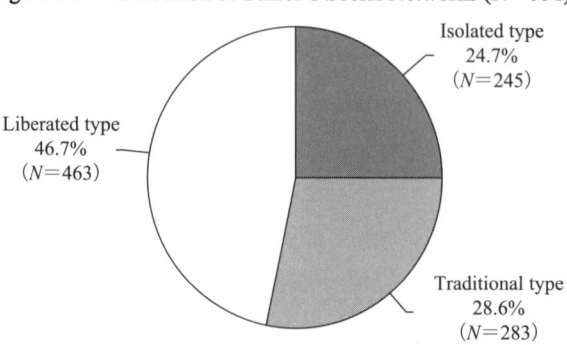

Figure 5-3 Distribution of Senior's Social Networks (*N* = 991)

Isolated type
24.7%
(*N*=245)

Liberated type
46.7%
(*N*=463)

Traditional type
28.6%
(*N*=283)

seniors' social networks in terms of size are shown in Table 5-5. Those having isolated types of social networks form an extremely small social network: each individual has a network of about three people. Elderly people with traditional-type networks are characterized by a large network of extended relatives and local community members. In the liberated type, people establish a relatively large network of friends, though the total social network size is the same as that of the traditional type. Figure 5-3 shows the distribution of the three types of social networks — "isolated," "traditional," and "liberated"— at 24.7%, 28.6% and 46.7%, respectively. The highest is the liberated-type social network, and the lowest is the isolated type, which does not match the image that elderly people are isolated. This result corresponds with the series of study results reported so far. Thus, many elderly people have many social networks with their friends in the center, which is classified as "liberated."

Next, a more detailed look is given to the three types of seniors' social networks. Table 5-6 indicates the frequency of interaction in the social networks of the elderly. The elderly people categorized as "isolated" are relatively low in the frequency of interaction with their children living elsewhere and friends. In contrast, those with a liberated type of social network interact with friends at high frequency. Table 5-7 shows the ratio of those having social networks within a 30-minute distance from their homes. Those having children living

Table 5-6 Seniors' Social Networks: Frequency of Interaction

(One visit or more a week: %)

	Children living elsewhere	Neighbors	Extended relatives	Friends
Isolated type	25.9	82.8	18.0	22.4
Traditional type	35.5	76.6	13.0	26.1
Liberated type	31.6	83.6	12.4	28.1

Table 5-7 Seniors' Social Networks: Spatial Distance

(30-minute distance or less: %)

	Children living elsewhere	Extended relatives	Friends
Isolated type	28.9	37.3	46.5
Traditional type	41.7	29.0	47.1
Liberated type	37.2	22.5	42.1

elsewhere, but within a distance of 30 minutes is lowest at 28.9% among seniors of the "isolated" type. In contrast, the ratio is relatively high among those of the "traditional" and "liberated" types. For the "isolated" type, their children are living far away from them, but they are more likely to have extended kin, including siblings living nearby, who may fulfill a substitute function. When seniors' social networks are examined in terms of three variables: size (no. of people), frequency of interaction, and geographical distance, the structure of each social network type can be represented as in Figure 5-4.

When comparisons are made among a traditional three-generation family, a single-person family, and a husband-wife family, how different are seniors' social networks? Table 5-8 shows the relations between seniors' family composition and the types of social networks.

Firstly, comparisons are made between a single-person family and a stem family (a senior living with her/his son and daughter-in-law). For elderly people living alone, many tend to have an isolated or liberated type of social network. In contrast, those living with their son and daughter-in-law are more

Figure 5-4 Types of Seniors' Social Networks (*N* = 991)

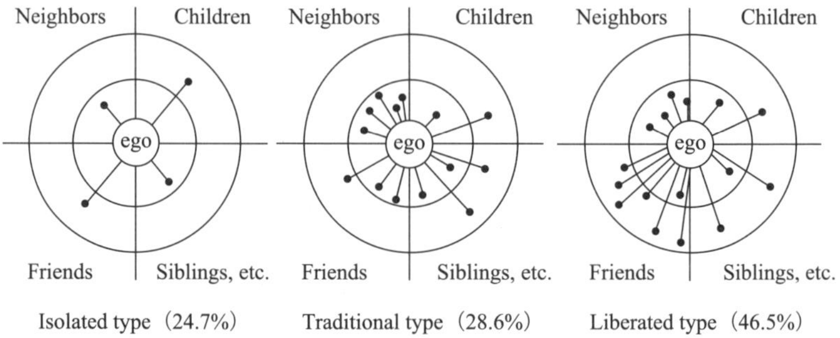

Isolated type (24.7%)   Traditional type (28.6%)   Liberated type (46.5%)

Note: The further network members are situated from the ego, the longer the geographic distance

likely to develop a traditional type of social network. In other words, there is no denying the fact that seniors living alone, rather than those from stem family, have fewer local community-oriented social networks, driving them into isolation from society. At the same time, however, it suggests that there is a possibility that they can undergo a change from the isolated type to the liberated type in which people enjoy rich social networks with their distant friends and kin.

Next, comparisons are made between seniors living with their son and his wife and those with their daughter and her husband. Elderly people living as a member of the traditional stem family, in which seniors are taken care of by their son and daughter-in-law under the same roof, are more likely to develop traditional —or local community-oriented— social networks. For those living with their daughter and her husband, however, a high percentage of them have

Table 5-8 Family Structure and Social Network Type of the Elderly (%)

	Isolated type	Traditional type	Liberated type	Total (*N*)
Living alone	29.5	24.2	46.3	100.0 (281)
Living with spouse only	20.6	26.6	52.8	100.0 (267)
Living with son's family	23.3	38.4	38.4	100.0 (146)
Living with daughter's family	20.3	31.9	47.8	100.0 (69)

a liberated type of social network. In recent years, living with a son and his wife under the same roof has been on the decline, while there has been an increase in the rate of those living with a daughter and her husband. The phenomenon of so-called "bilateral kinship" is now being observed (Ochiai, 1997). The results of analysis discussed in this chapter suggest that such a change in the traditional patrilineal family system can bring about changes in the structure and functions of social networks.

In other words, an increase in bilateral kinship in a family structure means a transition in seniors' social networks from traditional-type to liberated-type. The bilateral kinship and diversified social networks are compatible with each other, and it is expected that changes in the patrilineal family system will lead to a transition in seniors' social network structure from traditional-type to liberated-type.

6. Personal community building

This chapter explores the issue of isolated elderly people, from the viewpoint of social networks. Findings obtained from earlier studies and some data analysis can be generalized as follows:

(1) It cannot be said that elderly people are isolated in terms of social relationships. According to the analysis shown in this chapter, less than 30 % of the seniors surveyed are regarded as an "isolated" social network model. The existing studies concerning seniors' social networks also indicate that the image that elderly people are isolated is untrue. Some elderly people have traditional local-community-oriented networks, but many have developed broader social networks beyond the framework of a local community, with more frequent contact with distant friends. In short, elderly people have established diversified social networks centering on friends, rather than being isolated from society or only involved in traditional vertically

structured units, including a local community-based association.

(2) The transition in the family composition of the elderly from a traditional stem family, in which elderly parents live with their son and his wife, to a single-person family has brought about an increase in somewhat isolated social networks. As a whole, however, there is a change from the traditional type of social networks, in which social relationships are confined to a specific area, to the liberated type of networks centering on friends. In short, it is obvious that an increase in the number of elderly people living alone can give rise to their isolation from society. In reality, however, the transition in family structure is closely related to the formation of diversified social networks centering on friends. From this angle, we cannot assume that an increase in the population of elderly people living alone equals isolation from society.

(3) Bilateral kinship in a family structure has affected the social networks of the elderly. In the case of a three-generation family, there is a difference in the formation of seniors' social networks between those living under one roof with their son and daughter-in-law and those living with their daughter and son-in-law. A senior who is a member of the traditional patrilineal stem family tends to develop a traditional, local community-based social network (network confined to a specific area), whereas an elderly person who is living with her/his daughter and son-in-law is more likely to establish a liberated type of social network. In a word, bilateral kinship in a family structure is expected to give rise to a new type of social network centering on friends.

Based on these findings, certain observations can be made regarding the family structure of the elderly and their social networks.

The first observation concerns the isolation of elderly people. As mentioned at the beginning of this chapter, the family structure of the elderly is about to enter a new phase. In particular, there is a significant decrease in the proportion of a stem family, and a marked increase in that of a husband-wife family and single-person family. In these circumstances, what kind of social relationships that replace the traditional stem family system will be established by elderly people who are going to live alone or only with their spouses? As discussed in this chapter, the isolation of the elderly was not confirmed by earlier studies and data analysis. Instead, elderly people living alone tend to develop diversified social networks by actively interacting with distant friends while at the same time maintaining close relationships with their relatives and neighborhood, rather than being isolated from society or trapped within traditional local community-based relationships through getting involved in local activities/units only. For elderly people living alone, it is necessary to develop a social network that can be replaced with a family living under one roof. The discussions in this chapter suggest that there is a new type of close social relationship that is often a substitute for a family. As shown in Chapter 6 of this book, in which case studies confirmed the development of a new type of social relationship formed by seniors living alone, these discussions can draw a theoretical implications: For the elderly, living with their families has come to be one of the choices possible in their lifestyles, and such a change in family structure is bringing to the elderly new diversified social relationships centered on friends.

The second observation concerns an approach from the viewpoint of personal community. It is no longer taken for granted as being self evident that the elderly are taken care of by their children, as seen in the traditional stem family system. If it is unavoidable that senior citizens must choose living alone or only with their spouses, more emphasis should be placed on an "individual-based" social network. What is important for the elderly is how to form a unique social network suited to their own individuality, rather than the traditional family system where children take care of their elderly parents. People are living under broader social networks. For example, an elderly person "A" has a friend "B," whose friend is "C." In this way, individual elderly people seem to have boundless networks. From among those apparently boundless social networks, the most important social relationship that satisfies the daily needs of the elderly is the so-called "personal community" (Wellman et al., 1988). The personal community of the elderly may sometimes represent their families, relatives, or friends. In principle, however, it refers to a closer social relationship that can serve to meet the needs of life, beyond a relationship limited to a specific unit or community. This personal community will be very important when considering the life of elderly people. As observed in a growing population of elderly people living alone, it can be considered that broader social relationships, or personal community including professional services, will be the base of seniors' lives, while a family is regarded as one choice among several alternatives. Senior citizens should no longer be viewed as the socially vulnerable who need support from the special social relationship of a family. In considering what the society of the elderly ought to be in the future, if anything, it is critical to examine how elderly people live by themselves as much as possible and how they form social networks, with a focus on "each individual" as the main consideration.

Notes:

[1] In 1980, 52.2% of elderly people aged 65 or over were living with their married children, whereas the figure dropped to 32.8% in 1997 (Health and Welfare Ministry, 1998).

[2] In a study, a question was asked to those in their 30s and 40s about elderly people living with their married children. As of 1981, 45.9% of the respondents answered that it is better that elderly parents live with their son and daughter-in-law. However, the figure dropped to 39.7% in 1987, and to 35.2% in 1992. In contrast, 45.1% of respondents in 1992 answered that elderly parents and their children should live separately, showing a growing preference among the younger generation to live separately from their parents. When those in their 30s and 40s are asked about whether elderly parents, who are plagued by poor health, should live with their married children, 6.6% in 1981 said that elderly parents should live apart. The figure increased to 7.1% in 1987, and to 10.9% in 1992, showing a decline in public awareness of living with or taking care of elderly parents (Management and

Coordination Agency, 1992).

[3] For the concepts and methods of social networks, refer to Bott (1957), Burt (1984), Maeda (1992), Maeda & Meguro (1990), and Yasuda (1997).

[4] As for Japanese studies on social networks, see Fujisaki (1982), Matsumoto (1995), Nobe (1991), Nojiri (1974), Nozawa (1995), Ochiai (1993) and Otani (1995).

[5] The data used in this chapter is taken from a survey undertaken by the International Leadership Center on Longevity and Society concerning the living environment of the elderly. The survey was conducted in August 1995 on 1,200 men and women aged over 65 and living in their homes in Tokyo and 209 men and women aged over 65 who were living in complexes or institutions for elderly people. Non-institutionalized elderly were randomly selected from the Basic Resident Resister, and institutionalized elderly were chosen by senior-citizen institution/complex caretakers. There were 826 effective responses from non-institutionalized elderly and 169 from institutionalized elderly, with a collective rate of 70.6%. For detailed data, refer to the International Leadership Center on Longevity and Society (1995). This chapter provides the analysis results of the total number of the data (N = 995).

[6] The social networks of the elderly were divided into three types: the far right shows an isolated type of social networks; ①, traditional (local community-oriented) type; ② and

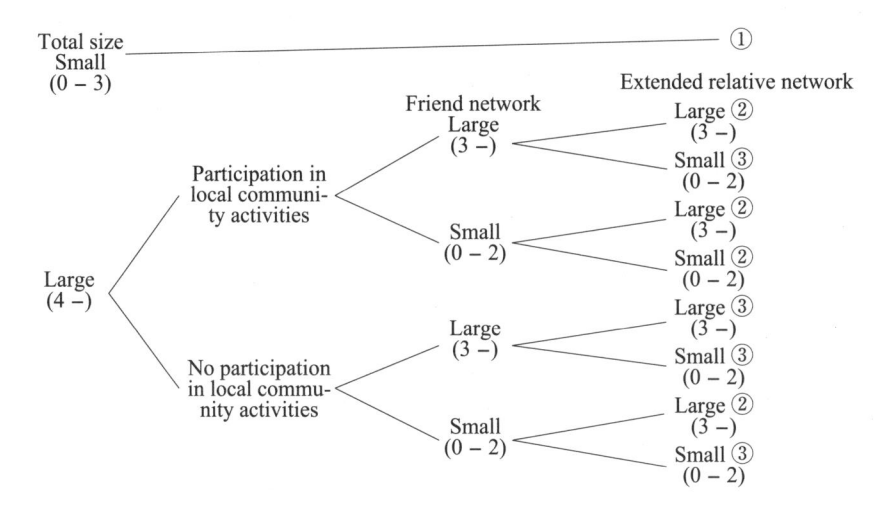

```
Total size                                                               ①
  Small ─────────────────────────────────────────────
  (0 – 3)                                         Extended relative network
                          Friend network                Large ②
                            Large                        (3 –)
                            (3 –)                       Small ③
              Participation in                           (0 – 2)
              local communi-                            Large ②
              ty activities                              (3 –)
                            Small                       Small ②
                            (0 – 2)                      (0 – 2)
  Large
  (4 –)                                                 Large ③
                            Large                        (3 –)
                            (3 –)                       Small ③
              No participation                           (0 – 2)
              in local commu-                           Large ②
              nity activities                            (3 –)
                            Small                       Small ③
                            (0 – 2)                      (0 – 2)
```

liberated; ③.

Personal Community of Elderly in Urban Situation

Chapter 6

1. Introduction

What may be of immediate help in studying informal human relationships in urban areas is two opinions on a community which have been utilized in urban sociology.[1] One of the two is "the community lost," a notion that along with massive social mobility resulting from industrialization, a traditional community falls apart, producing isolated individuals in cities. The other is "the community saved," a notion that even with progress in industrialization and urbanization, traditional kinship ties and neighborhood relationships will be retained for the continued maintenance of a relatively highly cohesive community. From the former standpoint, it is predicted that taken together a high possibility that the elderly will be separated from their spouses by death, more people living alone will be isolated from social organizations in urban areas. From the latter standpoint, meanwhile, it is predicted that few elderly people are isolated even in urban areas and that rather, many older persons will live in communities restricted in geographical mobility by traditional social norms. It is considered that there, they are strongly bound together through participation in *chonaikai*, or neighborhood associations, and other neighborhood activities, but that they enjoy the benefit of an established mutual-aid system and have the needs of their daily life met in specific regional groups.

These dichotomic opinions, however, are mere ideological "patterns" drawn from the results of many surveys taken so far, the contents of which are diversified depending on individual cases. In addition, my opinion about the community for the elderly is still a matter of assumption, and it is difficult to develop here elaborate models based on a new objective data analysis. In this chapter, I would like to introduce two cases of the elderly in urban areas and offer my hopothetical opinions about "the personal community" which can be drawn from them.[2,3]

2. Concept of personal community

The cases I will introduce in this chapter are concerned with older persons living in a *shitamachi*, or traditional commercial district called A in Tokyo.[4] My hypothesis prior to the survey was that since they reside in *shitamachi* quarters with many land-owners, the elderly are not isolated from each other but are in a relatively traditional and highly cohesive community. In fact, the A district retains its *shitamachi* aura; and it preserves many of traditional *shitamachi* characteristics that tightly packed shops and workshops with attached residences line narrow, winding streets. The traditional community is apparently kept alive as compared with *yamanote* areas. Incidentally, the *yamanote* (literally, "the foothills") is the districts and the traditions historically associated with *samurai* and now with the white-collar new middleclass. It is often contrasted with the *shitamachi*. In short, I imagined that the A district is an example of the aforementioned notion of "the community saved."

Of course, there are several other reasons why I pictured such an image of the A district. Firstly, the surveyed were older persons, and I feared that they found it no easy matter to physically move from one place to another even in contemporary society with developed means of transport and therefore, they tended to establish a regionally restricted group society. And secondly, it was predicted that partly due to Tokyo as the target of the survey, trends in migrants "from rural areas into urban centers," such as were seen nationwide during the high-growth era, were not necessarily true of the Tokyo metropolitan area and that both elderly people and their children had taken root in the area to form closely-knit group networks. However, this hypothesis of mine prior to the survey was not verified as far as case studies were concerned. Of course, it was a mere conjecture based on several interviews, and there is room for reexamination from quantitative data. Yet the results from my actual interviews, as will be discussed later, did not offer a social relationship which agrees with "the community lost" and "the community saved." True, neighbors and kinfolk, it was observed, were closely tied to each other in the A district as can be felt from a row of tightly packed shops and workshops with attached residences which retain much of *shitamachi* aura.

In this regard, the traditional concept of "the community saved," it seems, may be supported to some extent. But there was no obligated participation in *chonaikai* and no group-orientedness in the area observed. Rather, a top priority was given to the needs of the elderly's individual lives in maintaining neighborhood relationships and kinship ties. Also, social relationships were not regionally restrictive but were "selectively" sustained over a wide range of areas. In other words, the adequate image of the A district was, so to speak, that of "social relationships as social networks" which can be expressed as neither "isolated" nor "group-oriented." It should be noted, of course, that because of its nature of the surveyed area as Tokyo's *shitamachi*, the A district enjoys the privilege of closer neighborhood ties than other districts.

What is more, elderly people may face more limited mobility than young and middle-aged people since old age predictably forces physical weakness on them. But contrary to the general image so far observed, the elderly widen their scope of action by using such means of transport as buses and subways, or even "bikes!" in some cases. Furthermore, it was observed that they frequently mingle with friends and kins faraway also on the phone. In this sense, it seems that older persons maintain selective networks rather than they fall into oblivion in the traditional community or are isolated from society. To distinguish the community created by those selective networks from the conventional concept of the community, I will hereafter call it "personal community." In the cases that follow, I will introduce part of how such a "personal community" of the elderly is created.

3. Cases

Here I will deal with two cases of older persons living alone. These two cases are common in that both involve older persons of the same age. Despite the fact that they live by themselves, they have a wealth of friend networks by utilizing regional welfare centers for the aged. What they have created is not a regionally restrictive community strongly bound by the traditional territorial society and blood kins. Theirs, it is safe to say, is a personal community which is strongly colored by the selective character that they keep in touch with kinfolk and friends faraway space-wise by means of transport and by phone. But both are also good examples of "kins, and children in particular, living close by" within the networks which have created a subtle difference in expectations on formal administrative and professional services. In Case 1 shown below, Mrs. TW has formed a selective "personal community" and in addition, she has her adult children available in her neighborhood, human resources which can cope adequately with her daily life as well as emergency problems. Thus, she does not strongly feel the needs of administrative and professional services. In Case 2, meanwhile, Mrs. FU also has a "personal community" common to Mrs. TW in Case 1; however, she has no kinfolk available in her neighborhood, with her adult children living far away from her, and therefore, she strongly expects much of professional services such as a "home help."

114

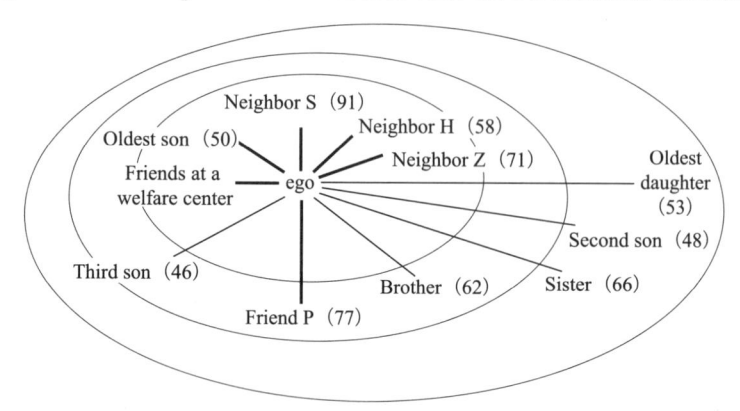

Figure 6-1 Case 1: Spatial Distribution of 83-Year-Old TW's Personal Community

```
                    Neighbor S (91)
                          |
        Oldest son (50)   |   Neighbor H (58)
              \           |  /
        Friends at a  —  ego — Neighbor Z (71)      Oldest
        welfare center  / | \                    — daughter
                       /  |  \                       (53)
                      /   |   \  Second son (48)
        Third son (46)    |    Sister (66)
                     Brother (62)
                    Friend P (77)
```

Note: The innermost oval indicates the area of her neighborhood; the second innermost oval represents an area she cannot reach on foot but can move back and forth the same day by train or car ; and the outermost oval shows an area she finds it difficult to move back and forth to on the same day. The bolder the lines in a network, the more frequently she has contact with people.

Case 1 (Mrs. TW)

A 83-year-old woman living by herself in a wooden apartment. She has relatives next door to her and has a wealth of friend and neighborhood networks.

Living alone, Mrs. TW seems to be consciously forward-looking in establishing social relationships. She is the case for an abundance of networks. Of the four children, her oldest son lives in a walking distance although her oldest daughter and her second oldest son live a long away from her. The oldest son is concerned about her and often steps in to see that everything is all right with her. Also, his wife and children (TW's grandchildren) sometimes visit her. Her third oldest son lives in the prefecture nearby and sometimes calls on her on his way back from work. All her sons have keys to her apartment so that they can look in at any time. It gives her a sense of security that they rush to her in case of emergency. She also mingles with her brother and relies on him but talks with him mostly on the phone since both are elderly.

Further characteristic of Mrs. TW's network of people is a wealth of neighbors and friends. Among them, she is particularly on friendly terms with Mrs. H, a 58-year-old woman who lives in the same apartment. Calling TW "granny, granny," Mrs. H comes in and has a little talk with her when she is free. For Mrs. H who does not have the mother, TW seems like her real mother. When Mrs. TW has pains in the legs and hip, Mrs. H sometimes goes to the hospital for her to pick her medicine. She goes to the hospital regularly. "She is like one of my family members. I am so pleased to be taken care of by her," Mrs. TW says, adding that she feels happy.

She has another important neighbor, a 91-year-old woman named S. Despite her old age, Mrs. S lives all by herself in a separate house in Mrs. TW's neighborhood. With her husband already dead, she has no children; nor does she have any relatives. She says she has her brother and his wife living in Tokyo but she hardly has contact with them. They just manage her money. Eighty-three-year-old TW is so concerned about 91-year-old S living alone and helps her with daily life. Living close by, she makes frequent visits to Mrs. S and has a talk over tea. She cares for Mrs. S in many ways; she helps Mrs. S get on and off the bus, take a bath and buy a bus ticket; also, she checks to see if she does her shopping all right. As seen above, 58-year-old H cares for 83-year-old TW, who in turn takes care of 91-year-old S. Mrs. TW thus has such a volunteer support system around her. Among such human relationships, Mrs. TW has one important friend who can always depend on 77-year-old Mrs. P, she got to know five years ago. They make phonecalls to each other every day to talk about daily happenings and consult with each other. They do not see each other frequently but occasionally they get together to pay homage to the shrine or to go shopping. Figure 2-1 shows Mrs. TW's personal community. In her case, her oldest son living close by is a decisive factor behind making her feel at ease. With this factor as a base, she has forged mutual aid in her neighborhood and communication networks with her friends. On the outskirts of her networks, she has her oldest daughter and relatives faraway, thus establishing an overall personal community transcending a certain space. Mrs. TW thinks she feels no need for experts' assistance at the moment.

Figure 6-2 Case 2: Spatial Distribution of 83-Year-Old FU's Personal Community

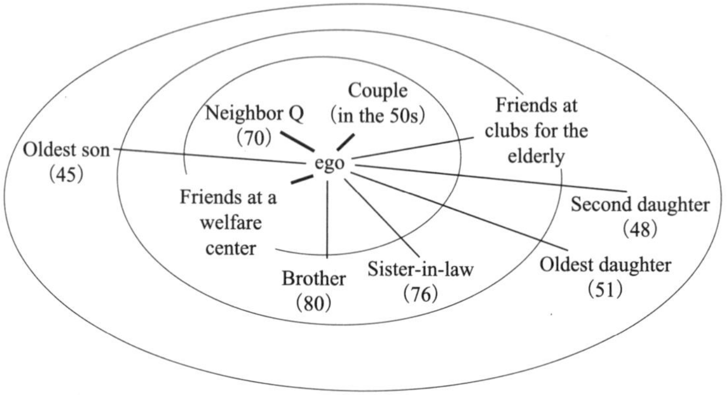

Note: The innermost oval indicates the area of her neighborhood; the second innermost oval represents an area she cannot reach on foot but can move back and forth to on the same day by train or car; and the outermost oval shows an area she finds it difficult to move back and forth to on the same day. The bolder the lines in a network, the more frequently she has contact with people.

Case 2 (Mrs. FU)

A 83-year-old woman living alone in a separate house. Has storehouses of friend and neighborhood networks and does feel little difficulty in her daily life. However, she has no adult children living nearby and she strongly expects much of professional support services, such as a "home help," regarding some of her daily-life problems.

Though 83 years old, Mrs. FU has no specific health problem; she has steady gait and has a wide scope of action. She has a good neighborhood and frequents a 70-year-old lady named Q close by. Also, she has a family of a middle-aged couple in their 50s living near to her who are concerned about her like their own relative. All of her three children live faraway, and she cannot see them so easily. They hope she will live together with them but she does not want to leave the place where she currently resides, saying that "I will feel lonely in a strange place where I have no friends." She gets two or three phonecalls a week from her oldest daughter living faraway. Of her relatives, the oldest daughter is most concerned about her. As she cannot see her children, Mrs. FU relies on her younger brother instead and seeks his advice about her important matters.

Her most important friends are those she sees in her neighborhood and at a welfare center for the aged. They are a network of friends through public organs in such a manner as to supplement kinship ties which tend to be less close. In this regard, the welfare center for the aged is an extremely important place for Mrs. FU to lead a delightful daily life. It is safe to say that the public organ plays a significant role for the elderly to form an informal network of friends. She says, however, that with all her children living far away, she sometimes feels inconvenienced in her daily life as a whole. If they lived close by, she could ask them to do what she wants them to; and she feels it hard to ask her neighbors and friends to do so. She does not want to trouble them to come and help her with a simple little thing like using insecticide. She says she does not hesitate to ask her children to do so. She cannot put New Year's decorations on a chest of drawers, change an old light bulb above for a new one and carry heavy stuffs up on the shelf.

On such occasions, she thinks, "I could have a professional home help available." She says she could feel free to ask a home help to do things. "I was told by my parents, 'Don't rely on others even if you rely on a cane!' and I am determined to do as many things as possible myself," she says. "Besides, I cannot very well tell important matters even to close neighbors as a proverb says: 'We cannot stop gossip,' " she continues. "I think I could rather tell a professional like a home help about important things," adding that "I would appreciate it very much if a home help could come and see me a week for house cleaning." Even if she has storehouses of neighbors and friends, Mrs. FU cannot feel free to tell them about her most important matters. In addition, she does not seem to want to be referred to by others a thing involving her privacy like her domestic matters. Therefore, she seems unable to feel free to ask her neighbors and friends to do what she can ask her own children to. That she does not have her adult children living near by and that she does not want her private matters made known by others constitute a barrier, thus making it impossible for her to establish a support network of people who take care of even her private daily matters. Thus, she places high expectations on professional home-help services. Figure 2-2 shows Mrs. FU's personal community.

Case 2 is in contrast to Case 1 in which Mrs. TW has her oldest son living close by and does not want much of professional support services like home-help services. It is undeniable that Mrs. TW's open-mindedness and relatively small privacy area enable an informal support network of people to be mobilized. But it is considered that a close relationship with her own children living near by gives her a sense of relief and makes her feel less necessary for professional support services like a home help. The needs for public organs like a welfare center and professional services in case of emergency are rather strong in Mrs. FU's case. A network of neighbors and friends works effectively to satisfy the emotional needs of a person, but a network of close relatives and parent-child relationships in particular, it seems, is more effective as a support for solving matters pertaining to privacy and daily trifles. It can be assumed that the tendency that when one cannot utilize a parent-child relationship, one had better leave to professionals rather than to his or her neighbors and friends who will satisfy his or her needs will be stronger.

4. Conclusions and discussion

The following are a more or less generalization of the research outcome of the personal community of the elderly living in Tokyo's *shitamachi* quarters.

(1) The elderly have an abundance of friend networks and also have established a network of friends at welfare centers and elderly people's clubs. Furthermore, they have created a network of distant friends by phone or by means of transport. To the elderly living alone without any relatives, welfare centers, which are public organs, play an extremely important role on forgetting about loneliness. But keeping company with friends at the welfare center is superficial and is meant only to enjoy conversations. It does not serve as an effective support for such issues as the elderly's family life. On the other hand, the elderly keep in close contact with a very few friends faraway to mutually seek private counseling and support.

(2) Time-honored *chonaikai* hardly functions; but there are relatively abundant neighborhood and networks of congenial elderly people which serve to provide mutual aid. Among the elderly are "those who aid and those who are aided;" and in some cases, there is established a voluntary age-group-wise mutual aid system under which those around 60 help those aged 80 and 80-year-olds help 90-year-olds with their daily lives.

(3) As far as case studies are concerned, no elderly persons totally rely on their kinfolk for a solution to their day-to-day problems. They selectively utilize a network of kins to satisfy the specific needs of their living. In this respect, a network of kinfolk, it is fair to say, shares its functions with a network of friends and neighbors. In particular, part of means functions like inheritance and financial management is shouldered by kinfolk, while shopping, support of overall daily life and many of emotional functions are shared by neighbors and friends; and thus, differentiated functions within the networks are clear.

(4) Expectations seem to be placed on professional services in the sense to make up for limited support functions of networks of relatives, friends and neighbors. The needs for professional services differ depending on age and health status, and also expectations of professional services are different from each other between the cases in which a network of relatives (especially that of children as seen from older parents is substantiated) and the case in which is otherwise.

The above four points are what I have learned from my several case studies. Based upon these points, I would like to make attempts at hypothetical considerations to go ahead with the discussions on the future personal community.

First, my case studies are essentially targeted for relatively healthy, older persons who are actively utilizing public organs like welfare centers for the aged and therefore, no cases which evoke the image of the so-called lonely old man could be found. I consider, however, that even among the elderly who are not isolated from society, formation of the network may perhaps be slightly different from that of a traditional *shitamachi* community. The first hypothesis which can derive from case studies is this. The elderly have formed social relationships, which should be termed a new "personal community" reflecting individuals' selective behavior; they do not live in a traditional community but they keep in close touch with friends faraway while making their contact with neighbors and relatives close by the basis of their networks. In the midst of rapid urbanization, the *shitamachi* community with neighborhood and kinship relationships as a basis has fallen apart; yet this is not to say that social relationships have collapsed. It cannot be said that the traditional community is retained; nor it can be said that the community has collapsed. There is established a social relationship, which should be called a "personal community," in which the elderly keep in close contact with friends and relatives faraway on the phone or by using such means of transport as buses and trains.

Second, formation of the personal community is diversified in its content. The second hypothesis which I can surmise here is concerned with a relationship between informal networks established by elderly people and their needs for public organs and professional services. To be more specific, even if the elderly could establish an abundance of social relationships, they would have different needs for formal administrative services depending on whether social relationships thus established are centered around kinfolk or neighbors or friends, or depending on how a variety of informal social relationships are joined together. Here I assume that even if the elderly can keep an abundance of social networks alive, their expectations on administrative services will differ considerably depending on whether there are "relatives living near by and adult children in particular" within the elderly's networks. As can be confirmed by cases cited above, even if older persons have formed an abundance of social networks and lead healthy daily lives, while keeping frequent contact with them, it is definitely important that they have those relatives living close by they can rely on when an emergency arises. They put more emphasis on relatives than on neighbors and friends as networks of people whom they can depend on at zero hour. Furthermore, it seems that of the relatives, they depend more on their adult children than on their brothers and sisters and distant relatives.

They seem to consider many of neighbors and friends are those who offer them superficial support for daily life and who satisfy the emotional needs particularly of conversations and socializing. Counseling on family matters and issues involving private lives is restricted only to relatives—many of whom are adult children and daughters in particular.[5] Thus, when they have no relatives near by, support functions to be shouldered by the networks are commissioned not to friends and neighbors but to formal professional services. As seen in the above Case 2, expectations on the "home help" are strong exactly among those who have no close relatives living close by. In this respect, it can be assumed that there are limitations on the interchangeability of the function of friends and neighbors with that of close relatives. To sum up, the second hypothesis is that when the elderly have no kinfolk living nearby and adult children in particular, their need for formal administrative services grows stronger. Yet the propriety of this hypothesis should be verified by further corroborative studies and should be still a matter of conjecture. Analyzing cases regarding the "personal community" and detailing models and theories by the development of quantitative surveys will be my future task to be tackled.

Notes:

[1] See Wellman (1979), for the theories of urban communities.

[2] My essential concern is with analysis of the family and the community by the use of a framework of research on social networks, an area of sociology. See Meguro (1989), for methodology of social networks in Japan.

[3] For recent urban research using the method of social networks, refer to Matsumoto (1992), Nozawa (1992), Nobe (1991), and Otani (1993).

[4] The survey was conducted as part of "Research and Study on Factors of the Living Environment for the Elderly (Chief: Prof. Takako Sodei at Ochanomizu Women's University)" Cases used in this chapter are part of the survey in which I was involved.

Using a similar framework I once analyzed the personal community of middle-aged women living in the outskirts of Tokyo and based on this, I made attempts at several hypothetical considerations. For more detail, see Maeda (1993).

[5] In Japan the vertical parent-child relationship seems to characterize the personal community. For this, see Maeda (1993), See also Wellman (1990).

Social Networks in Later Life and the Quality of Life

Chapter 7

1. Approach to the quality of life

In chapters 5 and 6, the social networks of the elderly was discussed from the view point of "personal community," and it was confirmed that personal community of the elderly living in urban areas is applicable to the "liberated" type of social networks centering on a broad network of geographically distant friends. Based on this knowledge, this chapter examines the relations between seniors' personal community and their quality of life. For this purpose, the subjective well-being of the elderly (morale scale), which was developed in the field of social gerontology in the U.S. and on which there are many experimental studies in Japan, is used as a measure of the quality of life to determine how quality of life is related to personal community.

2. Earlier studies

2.1 Quality of life and subjective well-being

In Japan, there have been many studies regarding the quality of life of the elderly. Among them, the Tokyo Metropolitan Institute of Gerontology has conducted pioneering research since late 1970. Representative research papers are those written by Maeda, et al. (1979, 1989), in which "subjective well-being" and "activity level" are dealt with to discuss the quality of life of the elderly and the morale scale is examined in quantitative terms, using Japanese data.

The morale scale was originally developed in the U.S. as a concept to express the morale of soldiers in the battlefield or the morale of company employees. Since then, the morale scale has been applied to studies of ageing. In particular, the PGC Moral Scale (Philadelphia Geriatric Center Morale Scale) created by Lawton (1972, 1975) has been studied in depth in Japan. The PGC Morale Scale consisting of 22 questions was revised and reduced to 17 questions. The revised version of the PGC Moral Scale came to be used widely for measuring the subjective 'well-being' of the elderly in Japan (Koyano & Ando, 2003).

The PGC Morale Scale provides a multidimensional approach to assessing the psychological state of the elderly. It consists of three factors: 1) people basically have a sense of satisfaction with themselves; 2) people think they have a place where they can be themselves; 3) people can accept an undeniable fact. As a result, seventeen items make up the revised PGC Morale Scale. Factor analysis of responses generated three factors: 'Agitation', 'Attitude toward own aging' and 'Lonely dissatisfaction (Lawton, 1972, 1975, Kayano & Ando, 2003).

The PGC Morale Scale has been repeatedly verified in Japan, and as with the results of P. Lawton, the presence of a factor structure has been confirmed.[1] As a result, the scale has been considered highly adaptable to studies on elderly people in Japan, and used in various experimental studies (Maeda et al., 1979; Maeda et al., 1989; Koyano & Ando, 2003).

2.2 Social networks and subjective well-being

Analyses revealed that the morale scale to measure subjective well-being, which is a dimension of the quality of life, is related to the lifestyle of the elderly, and light is gradually being thrown on a link between subjective well-being and social networks.[2]

Michiko Naoi indicates the relations between PGC Morale Scale and the social networks of elderly people. (Naoi, 2001) Naoi raised a question: Which interaction has more influence on the well-being of older people, interaction with kin or friends? (Naoi, 2001: 67). In response to this question, it was found that for men, interaction with friends contributes more to an increase in morale, while interaction with kin is more effective for women. Moreover, it was found that health is a variable highly relevant to the well-being of the elderly, for both men and women. Other important variables are household income and frequency of interaction with kin for women, and frequency of interaction with friends for men.

In addition, Ken Harada revealed a relation between the social networks of the elderly aged 75 or over who are living in urban areas, and their mental health (Harada et al., 2005). An analysis by Harada et al. indicates that for men, a network of friends living nearby helps increase the satisfaction they feel with their life, while for women, a network of kin living far away helps alleviate their distress and increases their life satisfaction. Although Harada's research did not use the PGC Morale Scale, it provides very valuable suggestions that show that the social networks of elderly people have significant effects on levels of satisfaction. In particular, what is most useful for the analysis in this chapter is that elderly people's involvement in the traditional type of social network with their kin living nearby does not always help improve their mental health. As indicated in the analyses in Chapter 5 and 6 in this book also indicates that a "liberated" type of personal community centering a network of friends, rather than a "traditional" type of personal community, is more effective in enhancing the quality of life of the elderly.

In addition, Masao Nobe, an urban sociologist, used data concerning women aged 60 to 79 who are living in Okayama City to find what factors determine the subjective well-being of elderly women (the PGC Morale Scale and life satisfaction). His analysis also suggests that the healthier they are and the more friends they have, the higher their subjective well-being is. It also found that elderly women who are involved voluntarily in religious organizations or sport/hobby groups show a high level of subjective well-being. Concerning these findings, Nobe explains that elderly women can have more friends by joining such groups or activities, and they feel a high subjective level of well-being by developing a broader network of friends (Nobe, 1999:119). Based on these earlier studies, it can be assumed that social networks are one of the variables that determine the quality of life of the elderly, and a network with friends in particular plays a significant role.

In reference to these earlier studies, this chapter explores the relation between social networks and the quality of life, by the following three processes.

The processes are (1) to reveal the distribution of the PGC Morale Scale of elderly people living in Tokyo, (2) to identify how the social networks of the elderly is related to the morale scale, and (3) to classify social networks into the three types: "isolated," "traditional" and "liberated" and to discover how each type of social network relates to the morale scale.

Through these processes, this chapter determines what relations there are between the three types of "personal community," described in Chapter 5, and the "quality of life" measured by subjective well-being.

3. Results [3]

3.1 Distribution of morale

The results of the analysis using the PGC Morale Scale are shown in Table 7-1. The samples were divided into two groups: the elderly at home and those at a nursing home. When morale is compared between the two groups, there was a significant difference at less than a 5% level in four out of the 17 items of the morale scale. When the values of well-being are added to obtain morale scores, the morale of the elderly at home scored 11.74, and 11.06 for institutionalized elderly, presenting a significant difference of less than 5%. (Table 7-2) The morale scores of all the samples average 11.63. This result corresponds to the results of earlier studies. For example, a survey conducted in the same area

Table 7-1 PGC Morale Scale Items (High-morale responses) (*N*=995)   (%)

	Elderly at home	Nursing-home elderly	Significance Level
1. Do things keep getting worse as you get older? (No)	70.1	64.2	*
2. Do you have as much pep as you had last year? (Yes)	62.5	51.2	***
3. Do you sometimes feel loneliness? (No)	75.6	68.9	**
4. Do little things bother you more in the past year or so? (No)	79.2	77.9	N.S
5. Do you see enough of your family, friends and relatives? (Yes)	88.9	84.0	*
6. Do you feel that as you get older, you are less useful? (No)	52.8	45.2	**
7. Do you sometimes worry so much that you can't sleep? (No)	72.6	69.5	N.S
8. Do you think that as you get older, things are better than you thought they would be? (Yes)	33.8	34.4	N.S
9. Do you sometimes feel that life isn't worth living? (No)	83.7	80.6	N.S
10. Do you sometimes feel that you are happier than when you were young? (Yes)	60.9	53.9	*
11. Do you have a lot to be sad about? (No)	84.5	85.3	N.S
12. Are you afraid of a lot of things? (No)	75.2	77.4	N.S
13. Do you get mad more than you used to? (No)	82.2	92.0	***
14. Is life hard for you most of the time? (No)	34.9	28.7	*
15. Are you satisfied with your life today? (Yes)	86.5	86.6	N.S
16. Do you take things hard? (No)	68.9	62.8	*
17. Do you get upset easily when you have something to worry about? (No)	79.0	81.4	N.S

Note: Statistical significance was determined by using the chi-square test. Significance level: ***<.01, **<.05, *<.10

Table 7-2 Average Morale Scores and Standard Deviation

	Morale scores	
	Average	Standard deviation
Elderly at home (*N* = 826)*	11.74	3.61
Nursing-home elderly (*N* = 169)	11.06	3.66
Total (*N* = 995)	11.63	3.63

Note: F value = 4.946   * Significance at 5% level

(Tokyo) by Michiko Naoi shows that morale scores of men and women are 11.9 and 11.7 respectively, which are approximately consistent with the data shown in this chapter (Naoi, 2001). In addition, the coefficient of reliability (Cronbach's coefficient alpha) of the morale scales used in this chapter is 0.802, showing high internal consistency. Therefore, it is appropriate to use the morale scale as a surrogate variable to present the quality of life of the elderly.

3.2 Distribution of health conditions and morale

Many earlier studies have revealed that the morale of the elderly is closely related to their health condition. In this chapter, it will be shown how social networks relate to morale when the health conditions of the elderly are controlled.

Table 7-3 shows the distribution of morale in the three types of personal community: "isolated," "traditional," and "liberated." [4] Morale is lowest among those with an isolated type of personal community, while it is highest among

Table 7-3 Morale Scores by Social Network Type of the Elderly

	Morale score ***	Standard deviation	N
Isolated type	10.51	3.99	245
Traditional type	11.93	3.50	283
Liberated type	12.05	3.35	463
Total	11.63	3.61	991

Note: F value = 16.50   *** Significance at 1% level

Table 7-4 Health Conditions of the Elderly

	% (N)
Go out alone by bicycle, car, or bus	83.4 (807)
Active at home and in the neighborhood, but cannot go far alone	11.3 (109)
Active to some degree	2.1 (20)
Get out of bed but not active	2.0 (19)
Spend a lot of time in bed	1.0 (10)
Bedridden	0.3 (3)
Total	100.0 (968)

Table 7-5 Correlation between Social Network Types and Morale by Health Condition [1]

	Morale scores *** [2]			
	Good health		Poor health	
	Average (SD)	N	Average (SD)	N
Isolated type	10.82 (3.75)	164	9.85 (4.38)	81
Traditional type	12.23 (3.30)	239	10.31 (4.10)	44
Liberated type	12.26 (3.24)	402	10.70 (3.80)	61
Total	11.96 (3.41)	805	10.24 (4.13)	186

Notes: 1) Good health: "go out alone by bicycle, car or bus" (83.4%).
Poor health: "active at home and in the neighborhood, but cannot go far alone" (11.3%), "active to some degree" (2.1%), "get out of bed but not active" (2.0%), "spend a lot of time in bed" (1.0%), and "bedridden" (0.3%).
2) F value = 16.50   *** Significance at 1% level

those with the "liberated" type personal community. The ranking of types, from highest to lowest, is liberated (12.05), traditional (11.93) and isolated (10.51).

Table 7-4 shows the distribution of health conditions. Many of the elderly used as data in this chapter are in good health. Of the subjects, 83.4% go out alone on a bicycle, by car or bus, indicating that they are very active. On the other hand, 11.3% are active at home and in the neighborhood, but cannot go far alone, and the remaining 5.4% are a total of those who are active to some degree, those who get out of bed but are not active, those who spend a lot of time in bed, and those bedridden.

Table 7-5 shows the relations between each type of social networks and morale by dividing the subjects into two groups according to the level of health condition: those who can go out alone by bicycle, car or bus are regarded as being in "good health" and the remainder are in "poor health." When the total scores of morale are compared between the two groups, those in good health score 11.96, and those in poor health 10.24; it is evident that elderly people in good health have a higher level of morale. In other words, the better health conditions they are in, the higher subjective level of well-being they show. Concerning the distribution of morale by personal community type among those in good health, the highest in morale is a "liberated" type of personal community (12.26), which is followed by "traditional" (12.23) and "isolated" (10.82). The same tendency was observed among the elderly in poor health: the highest in morale is the "liberated" type, followed by "traditional" and "isolated." Even when the level of health is controlled, there is a significant relation between the three types of personal community and morale. (F value = 16.50, Significant at 1% level)

Thus, it can be said that a "liberated" type of personal community, regardless of health level, tends to show higher subjective level of well-being.

3.3 Personal community and subjective well-being

Table 7-6 shows the multiple regression analysis of the effects of seniors' social network measures on morale. To identify relative effects, "morale scores" were regarded as dependent variables, and seniors' social network measures, which are independent variables, were divided into four: "children living elsewhere," "network of relatives," "network of neighbors," and "network of friends." The analysis indicates that there are two independent variables that have significant effects on the morale of the elderly at less than a 5% level: the size of a friend-based network and the frequency of interaction with friends. In short, the larger the friend-based network is, the higher the morale score ($\beta = .135$). And, the higher the frequency of interaction with friends is, the higher the morale score ($\beta = .199$). Another point worth noting is that the size of the neighbor network also positively affects the morale of the elderly. As shown in Table 7-5, a "traditional" type of personal community, next to "liberated," is high in morale. This is because for the elderly who find it more difficult to travel around than young and middle-aged people, a network of neighbors is an important factor in enhancing the quality of life when they do not have a specific friend-based network. Thus, among the social network measures, a friend-based network and neighbor network have more influence

Table 7-6 The Effects of Seniors' Social Network Measurement on Morale

	Standardized coefficient (β)	t value
Children living elsewhere		
Geographical distance (far)	−.183	−1.786*
Frequency of interaction (high)	−.184	−1.790*
Network of relatives		
Size (large)	.021	.336
Geographical distance (far)	.055	.566
Frequency of interaction (high)	.133	1.413
Network of neighbors		
Size (large)	.127	1.908*
Frequency of interaction (high)	−.060	−.964
Length of relationship (long)	.056	.795
Network of friends		
Size (large)	.135	2.024**
Geographical distance (far)	.065	.844
Frequency of interaction (high)	.199	2.578**
Length of relationship (long)	.134	1.899*
Constant		4.605***
R^2	.080	
F value	2.770***	
N	246	

Note: Significance level: ***<.01, **<.05, *<.10
R^2 represents an adjusted value.

on morale, and it cannot be said that a network of kin is significantly effective in enhancing the morale of the elderly.

Table 7-7 shows the multiple regression analysis of personal community's relative effects on morale scales. With a "liberated" type of personal community used as a dummy variable in contrast with the "traditional" and "liberated" types, analysis was made of the effects of a "liberated" type of personal community on morale scores. There are eight controlled variables: "institutionalized," "length of residence (long)," "health condition (good)," "academic background (high)," "age (high)," "gender (male)," "occupation (employed)" and

Table 7-7 Multiple Regression Analysis of Morale Scores

	Standardized coefficient (β)	t value
Institutionalized	−.015	−.373
Length of residence (long)	0.36	1.091
Health condition (good)	.145	4.936***
Network type (liberated)	0.68	2.138**
Academic background (high)	.081	2.484**
Age (high)	.022	.632
Gender (male)	.052	1.547
Occupation (Employed)	.116	3.418***
Living alone	−.005	−.112
Constant		4.900***
R^2	.065	
F value	8.611***	
N	985	

Note: Significance level: ***<.01, **<.05, *<.10
R^2 represents an adjusted value.

"living alone." The analysis discloses that even when the remaining variables are controlled, a "liberated" type of personal community presents higher morale scales. Other significant variables at less than a 5% level are "health condition," "academic background," and "occupation." In general, it can be said that employed elderly people who are in better health, have a higher academic background and form a "liberated" type of personal community tend to present higher subjective levels of well-being. In terms of personal community, senior citizens who have a broader network of friends and aggressively interact with distant friends tend to lead a higher quality of life, regardless of socioeconomic status or health condition.

4. Personal community and the quality of life

The following analysis findings concerning the relations between social networks and subjective well-being among the elderly, which is the theme of this chapter, can be summed up as follows:

(1) With regard to the relations between social network measures and morale scores, a network of friends shows significant relevance. In particular, elderly people who have a larger network of friends and interact with friends at a higher frequency tend to show higher morale scores. In addition, the larger a network of neighbors is, the higher the morale scores.

(2) When personal community is divided into the three types of "isolated," "traditional," and "liberated," morale scores are lowest among those with an "isolated" type of personal community, and highest among those with a "liberated" type. In decreasing order of morale, they are "liberated" > "traditional" > "isolated."

(3) A glance at analysis of variance with the health conditions of the elderly controlled reveals a significant relevance between personal community and morale. Regardless of health condition, the formation of the "liberated"-type personal community contributes to enhancing the subjective well-being of the elderly.

(4) In a multiple regression analysis with morale scores as dependent variables, the relative effects of socioeconomic variables, health condition and personal community on morale were examined. It was found that elderly people who are in better health, have a better academic background, and have a job are more likely to show a higher level of morale.

(5) Even when socioeconomic variables are controlled in the multiple regression analysis, those with the "liberated" personal community tend to present a higher level of morale.

(6) These findings indicate that elderly people who form a "liberated" type of personal community —i.e. have a broad friend-based network— tend to show a high subjective level of well-being.

Before concluding this chapter, some observations should be considered regarding personal community and the quality of life on the basis of these findings.

Firstly, the same findings as those of earlier studies were found concerning relations between social networks and subjective well-being. What is notable is that a network of friends tends to enhance the subjective well-being of the elderly. As mentioned at the outset, some earlier sociological studies have revealed that building a network of friends has a positive effect on the quality of life of the elderly, including subjective well-being and mental health (Naoi, 2001; Nobe, 1999; Harada et al., 2005). The analysis in this chapter presents the same results: the quality of life of elderly people measured by subjective well-being can be enhanced by developing an extensive network of friends.

Secondly, a network of neighbors, in addition to a network of friends, is also an important variable for elderly people. Even in urban areas where people have poor interpersonal relations with neighbors, a network of neighbors plays a key role in the everyday life of those elderly people who find it difficult to travel due to physical health. In short, a neighborhood network is as important as a support resources for elderly people. It will be an important challenge to determine the differences between the function of friend-based networks and that of neighborhood networks, as discussed with case studies in Chapter 6. From a public policy perspective, environmental planning that allows elderly people to establish a network of distant friends and policies to form a community that enables the reconstruction of neighborhood networks will be increasingly important in ageing urban areas.[5]

The last observation concerns the methods of social network studies. The qualitative analyses and systematic classification of social networks will be important in determining welfare and urban policies. As observed in the analysis of this chapter, it can be said that the three types of personal community, developed through urban studies by the Canadian sociologist Barry Wellman (1979), show a certain level of effectiveness in relations between each type of social network and subjective well-being. In particular, the positive effects of the "liberated" personal community on subjective well-being are stimulation in regard to further community studies on the elderly. In Japan, there are a number of analyses concerning the impact of quantitative variables of social networks on subjective well-being and satisfaction with life. However, only a few studies have been conducted in terms of classification of social networks. Regarding relations between qualitative analyses of social networks and support, pioneering research was conducted by C. Wenger, using case studies on social networks of elderly people living in Wales, UK (Wenger, 1996). In considering what kinds of welfare services and support system should be provided [6], important challenges in Japan will be not only to quantitatively determine social networks but also to classify social networks through a number of qualitative analyses.

Notes:

[1] Concerning the quality of life measured only by subjective well-being, Sugisawa (2002) argues that objective measures should be used. In this respect, there is a limit to the application of the PGC Morale Scale as a variable of the quality of life. For the theme of this chapter: "social networks and the quality of life," further examination is necessary using objective measures involving agism and other cultural factors.

[2] Recent social epidemiological studies have also indicated that social networks affect the health of people and the prevalence rate for diseases. For instance, Berkman and Kawachi (2000) revealed that social networks (i.e. social capital) determine the health level of people. Social epidemiology can be called social medicine for groups, but cooperation is expected between sociology and social epidemiology for conducting applied research. Such efforts can lead to further developments into sociology in medicine, a field of medicine, beyond the conventional framework of the sociology of medicine (Syme, 2000). For other studies about social networks and health, refer to Berkman (1995), Kawachi et al. (1999), and Kawachi and Berkman (2003). For a Japanese version of these studies, see Okado & Hoshi (2002) and Kondo (2004).

[3] As in chapters 5 and 6 of this book, the data used in this chapter is from a study on life environment of the elderly conducted by the International Leadership Center on Longevity and Society (1995). The survey was conducted in August 1995 on 1,200 men and women aged 65 and over who are living in their homes and 209 men and women aged 65

and over who are living in a housing complex or institutions for elderly people. For detailed data, refer to Note 5 in Chapter 5. This chapter presents the results of analysis with the total number of data (N=995).

[4] The classification of personal community into three types is the same as in Chapter 5. For detailed information on the classification method, refer to Note 6 in Chapter 5.

[5] With ageing in urban areas, a local community-based approach will be of growing importance in welfare for the elderly. The field of urban engineering has already proposed community-based planning and has begun to adapt findings of sociological studies. In this respect, refer to Koizumi et al. (2001). For the sociological approach, see Asakawa & Takahashi (1992).

[6] See Inoue (2004) for a recent study that discusses "welfare community as a network," from the perspective of social networks.

Chapter 8

Summary and Conclusion

1. Summary

As mentioned in the preface, this book aims to identify the factors that contribute to enhancing the quality of later life and those that lead to an active life after mandatory retirement, with the main focus on the effects of post-retirement "jobs" and "social networks." The basic questions discussed in this book can be summarized as follows.

The first question concerns whether the notion of active ageing can be seen in the post-retirement life planning of Japanese people.

Chapter 2 mainly explores Japanese people's attitudes toward diversified lifestyles and occupational career formation in later life, with middle to later life regarded as the second career formation stage. As a result, findings show a clear change in the meaning of mandatory retirement.

During the decade from 1991, the percentage of those who associate financial difficulties with mandatory retirement increased, indicating that middle-aged and older people were placed in a severe employment situation. On the other hand, however, there was an increase in the number of those having positive images of mandatory retirement, saying that it has brought a new world to them or that they have a lot of free time again. In this respect, a new post-retirement culture is now being created, in which mandatory retirement is viewed positively as a vital turning point in a course of life and as the second stage of career development.

The period of the 1990s was characterized by the harsh employment environment for middle-aged workers. However, it was found that many people had positive attitudes toward mandatory retirement with the intention of developing a variety of careers. While middle-aged employees were buffeted by the "lost decade" of the 1990s in terms of occupational career formation, they are contributing to the creation of a new post-retirement culture. Despite an economically difficult social environment - commonly known as the "second long-term economic slump" (Tominaga & Miyamoto 1998), middle-aged employees tend to regard mandatory retirement positively and respond to it in a flexible manner. This means that the norm of active ageing, where the concept is to lead an active life after mandatory retirement, rather than viewing retirement in a negative light, has come to be established.

Therefore, it can be said that elderly people can play a proactive role in creating a welfare society in a broad sense, through continued work or active involvement in the local community, rather than just accepting their status as a target of welfare.

The second question is about how older people adapt themselves to mandatory retirement. Can continued work contribute to enhancing the quality of life?

To this question, the analysis presented in Chapter 4 answers to a certain extent. The data analysis shows that men, who are more likely to remain in the workforce after mandatory retirement than women, make their life adjustments after mandatory retirement through continued work. In contrast, women, who are more inclined to leave the labor market or continue to work as non-regular employees after mandatory retirement, make their life adjustments through long-term relationships with friends or closer relationships with neighbors, taking advantage of local community resources.

There seems no major difference between men and women in the quality of life after mandatory retirement. However, there is a gender difference in the process of life adjustments after retirement, during which so-called "bridge jobs" and "involvement in the local community" play an important role in the process of life adjustments for both men and women, and contributes to the quality of later life.

As a result, continued work can have positive effects on the quality level of the post-retirement life among Japanese men.

How can gender differences in the process of mandatory retirement be explained from a sociological viewpoint? First, mandatory retirement can be examined in terms of "continuity" in a course of life. In Japan, men tend to maintain their motivation through the continuity of careers by remaining in the labor market after retirement, whereas women tend to maintain continuity via relationships with friends and the local community. The "continuity" and "discontinuity" of those life events can be true of the men and women targeted in this book. Men maintain the continuity of their life course by remaining in the workforce after mandatory retirement, making their life adjustments to the discontinuity of a life course, or mandatory retirement.

In contrast, women, rather than men, are less likely to remain in the labor market after retirement, but they tend to maintain closer relationships with their friends and the local community that they have already developed. In other words, women seem to maintain the "continuity" of a life course by taking advantage of informal network resources, such as friends and neighbors, rather than through continued work. Although men and women experience the shared "discontinuity" event of mandatory retirement in the gendered life-world, it is presumed that there is a gender difference in maintaining "continuity" underlying a course of life.

The third question of this book is about how a social network relates to the quality of later life and what kind of social network can contribute to life quality enhancement. This question is addressed by the analyses conducted in chapters 5 to 7.

The chapters 5 and 6 of this book, in which a social network of older people is regarded as a "personal community," confirm that the personal community of the elderly living in urban areas is applicable to the "liberated" type of social networks, centering on a broad network of geographically distant friends.

Based on this knowledge, Chapter 7 explores the relations between seniors' personal community and their quality of life. For this purpose, the subjective well-being of the elderly (morale scale), which was developed in the field of social gerontology in the U.S. and on which there are many ongoing experimental studies in Japan, is used as a measure of the quality of life to determine how quality of life is related to personal community.

As a result, older people's network of friends shows the most significant relation between a social network and morale. In particular, elderly people who have a larger network of friends and interact with friends at a higher frequency tend to show higher morale scores. In addition, the larger a network of neighbors, the higher the morale scores.

When personal community is divided into the three types of "isolated," "traditional" and "liberated," morale scores are lowest among those with an "isolated" type of personal community, and highest among those with a "liberated" type. In decreasing order of morale, they are "liberated" > "traditional" > "isolated."

A glance at analysis of variance with the health conditions of the elderly reveals a significant relevance between personal community and morale. Regardless of health condition, the formation of the "liberated"-type personal community contributes to enhancing the subjective well being of the elderly.

These findings indicate that elderly people who form a "liberated" type of personal community - i.e. have a broad friend-based network - tend to help enhance the quality of life.

However, it was confirmed that a network of neighbors, in addition to a network of friends, is also an important variable for older people. Even in urban areas where people tend to have poor interpersonal relations with neighbors, a network of neighbors plays a key role in the everyday life of those elderly people who find it difficult to travel due to physical health. In short, a neighborhood network is as important as a support resources for older people. It will be an important challenge to determine the differences between the function of friend-based networks and that of neighborhood networks, as discussed with case studies in Chapter 6. Consequently, policies where environmental planning allows elderly people to establish a network of distant friends and policies designed to form a community that enables the reconstruction of neighborhood networks will be increasingly important in ageing urban areas.

2. General and policy implications

Based on the findings obtained through the experimental studies of this book, policy implications can be proposed for an ageing society with fewer children. The three policy implications are as follows.

2.1 Active ageing and citizenship

The first implication is to attach importance to the concept of "active ageing." This issue was examined mainly in chapters 2 ,3 & 4 of this book, by conducting experimental analyses of the development and design of occupational careers. Certainly, elderly people have weaker physical strength than when they were young, but their health conditions and lifestyles vary so widely that it is hard to lump them together under one label as the "elderly." Although their health is declining, elderly people should not be protected in every way as being socially vulnerable. It is necessary to view them as those who can fulfill their roles - even partially - as contributing members of society. The findings of analyses conducted in this book indicate the need for perceiving the activities of elderly people as being essential to the establishment of social networks, including volunteer and local community activities, rather than considering seniors' activities only from the viewpoint of "employment." In other words, elderly people should be viewed from the perspective of developing social networks, including local community or non-profit organization activities and other activities outside companies. In policy terms, it will be more important to form social foundations not only for elderly people who receive support but also for seniors who provide support.

In this respect, the perspective of citizenship takes on considerable importance. This does not refer to the protection of seniors as being socially vulnerable, as observed in traditional welfare states. It means citizenship that grants the right and duty to be a contributing member of society regardless of age. A requirement of citizenship is to ensure that older people can get involved in decision-making processes. For instance, a system will be needed that allows elderly people to directly participate in the planning of regional activities by providing them with a variety of information, ranging from employment, working conditions, housing, education, to health. Such need for information sharing and involvement in decision making is a common thread shared with citizenship for young people today (Miyamoto 2005). Central to this issue is not to exclude elderly people from society but to include them in society. Given more diversified lifestyles in later life and higher risks in a transition to a later stage of the life course, as described later, importance should be attached to policies that abolish age discrimination and provide willing elderly workers with opportunities to work.

2.2 Life course perspective and employment/labor policies

The second implication is to view active ageing from a life course perspective. As issues of ageing and some life course policies taken in major European countries, some countries have started to increase the retirement age of elderly workers and inaugurated a policy of redistributing work time in a life course, in response to a prolonged working life. Such a policy enables changes of a life cycle, from a typical life cycle in which people work long hours in the prime of life and then have their working hours significantly reduced after mandatory retirement in later life to a life cycle that allows more flexible retirement in a life plan to redress the balance between private life and work time. In other words, as measures to tackle ageing issues, some European countries have shifted direction toward enhancing the flexibility of the entire working life by allowing people to design their occupational careers in regard to their later life while they are young or in the prime of their lives. Given such a situation, the Japanese government should also take measures against ageing based on the idea that ageing does begin early in life, not in later life. The ageing issue needs to be tackled from the perspective of a life course: a lifestyle in later life is considered a direct extension of a lifestyle chosen in early in life. The life-course perspective that ageing does not refer only to a certain period of time (later stage) of life course and that the issue of ageing should be addressed by designing an occupational career in early life will be an important requirement for society to support active ageing.

The life course approach of the transition to the later stage is not applied only to employment policy and other specific fields. For ageing policy, a life-course perspective and holistic approach to support working life will be required.

To this end, a comprehensive employment/labor policy can be proposed from the perspective of a lifelong career, which is based on the concept of redistributing the lifetime.

In this sense the model proposed by German economist G. Schmid could be applied to the present book's active ageing policy proposed from a life course perspective (Schmid 2000; Schmid 2002).

Schmid's model consists of five kinds of labor market transitions: (1) transitions between education/training and employment, (2) transitions between part-time and full-time employment, dependent versus self-employment, or a combination of the two patterns, (3) transitions between unpaid work at home or in private activities and paid work in labor market activities, (4) transitions between unemployment and employment, and (5) transitions between employment and temporary incapacity for work, including a flexible retirement.

The five areas of the Schmid model are linked by reliable "bridges." Those individual areas secure a guarantee of employment. It is presupposed that even if people temporarily leave the workforce for child rearing or nursing care, they can return to the labor market as paid workers. Likewise, the model facilitates shifts between paid work and unpaid work in various phases of life, ranging from transitions to education, transitions to incapacity for work resulting from unexpected illness or accidents, or flexible transitions to retirement in a later life, thus enabling the designing of individual people's life courses by transitions between paid work and unpaid work (Schmid 2000; Schmid 2002).

In this model, the notion of "labor" is not narrowly interpreted as employment/labor, but its meaning is extended to cover the unpaid work that is generally shouldered by women, such as unpaid child rearing and nursing care. In addition, the model gives consideration to gradual transitions to retirement from the labor market through flexible moves between community activities and employment in a later stage of the life course. Schmid notes that ending and preventing unemployment is the only purpose of welfare services today. However as characterized in the artist labor markets, he says, labor represents some important meaning, or artists' own lives, as well as revenue raising activities, and when both are mutually related, it can be called the welfare today (Schmid 2000; 29). Thus, he argues that a welfare society can be created by pursuing the possibility that people can make an educated choice from among diversified working patterns (paid or unpaid; or dependent or self-employment).

Again, such a labor market transition model neither focuses attention on a later stage of the life course nor views employment as the only labor pattern. It is an integrated policy model for working life that perceives labor in a broad sense to cover not only employment but also household work, community activities and other unpaid work, with working life from an early stage of the life course in view [1]. In this respect, the Schmid model can be evaluated as being an important model for a comprehensive ageing policy that allows diversified life courses from an early stage to later stage of the life course.

2.3 Diversified lifestyles in a later life and lifelong learning policy

The third implication concerns a perspective on "diversified" lifestyles in a later life. The massive retirement of the so-called baby boomers starting from 2007 heralds the arrival of a full-fledged aged society. The baby boomers, although forming a large cohort, have a diversity of lifestyles. Some are eager to remain in the workforce even after their mandatory retirement age, and others are willing to enjoy their retirement living on a pension. Thus, the advent of an aged society will bring about more diversified lifestyles. As revealed in the analyses conducted in this book, people aged 60 and over can work in various ways, depending on their assets, savings, will to work, and working environment. Therefore, there is no specific working life model for career formation in a later life. The model of active ageing is predicated on the diversified lifestyles of elderly people, depending on their health or economic conditions. Seen in this light, individual elderly people need to look for working patterns or lifestyles most suitable for themselves.

Especially in Japan, lifelong learning will be an important policy, as a measure to break the standardized lifelong career pattern that baby boomers have followed. Following the phased increase of the age at which a pension is payable to 65, it is indispensable for Japan to create a system that provides opportunities for elderly people to preserve their vocational abilities or newly develop their capabilities, rather than a system entirely focusing on life after the receipt of a pension. In other words, active citizenship should be considered from the aspects of both "right" and "duty." In return for enhancing their employability, elderly people have the duty to contribute to society by remaining in the labor market or getting involved in volunteer activities. For that purpose, lifelong learning that demands vocational capability will be one of the mainstay of education policy in terms of citizenship.

Furthermore, lifelong learning plays a significant role in policies designed to promote diversity in active ageing. As in the above-mentioned transitional labor market model, the establishment of an education system under which people can enjoy lifelong learning regardless of age will be an important strategy not only for facilitating employment but also encourageing diversity in active ageing, such as involvement in NPO activities or self-employment. It will become a principal pillar of Japan's education policy to provide recurrent education to middle-aged and elderly persons, through which workers, full-time homemakers, other adults from various backgrounds as well as young people can have opportunities to receive education for capability development or cultural enrichment.

Note

[1] Miyamoto (1999) has found a direction of labor-market reforms in Schmid's "transition model" when analyzing the formation of a welfare state in Sweden. In her argument about a reduction in working hours and the restructuring of labor, Tanaka (2006) gives a broader definition of the concept of labor and introduces new attempts made in Germany, which is very thought provoking in the sense that she proposes the restructuring of the way people work.

Referrences

Chapter 1

Atchley, R. and Barusch, A., 2004, "Social Forces and Ageing: An Introduction to Social Gerontology" (tenth edition), Wadsworth.

Cumming, E. and Henry, W., 1961, "Growing Old: The Process of Disengagement", Basic Books.

Elder, G, H., 1974, "Children of the Great Depression: Social Changes in Life Experiences", University of Chicago Press.

European Commission, 1999, "Towards a Europe of all ages", Brussels: European Commission.

Funatsu,M., 2003, *"Koureisha no Jiga* (Self-identity of Older People)", Shoji Tsuji and Mamoru Funatsu ed., *"Eijingu no Shakaishinrigaku* (Social Psychology of Ageing)", Hokuju Shuppan, 41-55.

Hall, A. and Wellman, B., 1985, "Social Networks and Social Support," Cohen, S. and Syme, L. ed., "Social Support and Health", New York: Academic Press, 23-41.

Hamaguchi,K., 1999, *"EU ni okeru Koyouseisaku to Shakaihoshou* (Employment Policies and Social Security in the EU)", *"Kaigai Shakaihoshou Jouhou* (The Review of Comparative Social Security Research)", Vol. 128, National Institute of Population and Social Security Research, 62-74.

——, 2000, *"EU Shakaiseisakushisou no Tenkan* (Transformation of Social Policies in the EU)", *"Kikan Roudouhou* (Labor Law Quarterly)", Vol. 194, Sogo Rodo Kenkyusho, 105-128.

——, 2003, *"EU no Roudou・Shakaiseisaku to Nihon eno Inpurikeeshon* (Labor and Social Policies in the EU and Their Implications for Japan)", *"Kikan Kaigaijouhou Houkoku* (Quarterly Overseas Information Bulletin of Overseas)", Vol. 7, Japanese Ministry of Health, Labour and Welfare, 34-55.

Havighurst, R. 1954, "Flexibility and the Social Roles of the Retired," American Journal of Sociology, Vol. 59, No. 2, 309-311.

Hooyman, N. and Kiyak, H., 1995, "Social Gerontology: A Multidisciplinary Perspective" (fourth edition), Allyn and Bacon.

International Labor Organization (ILO), 2002, "An Inclusive Society for an Ageing Population: The Employment and Social Protection Challenge. The Second world Assembly on Ageing", Madrid.

Johnson, M., Bengtson, V., Coleman, P. and Kirkwood, T., 2005, "The Cambridge

Handbook of Age and Ageing", Cambridge University Press.

Kaneko, I., 1998, *"Koureishakai to Anata —Fukushishigen o dou tsukuruka* (Aged Society and You: How to create welfare resources)", NHK Shuppan.

Koyano, W. and Ando, T., 2003, *"Shinshakai Rounengaku —Shiniaraifu no yukue* (New Social Gerontology: Future direction of senior life)", World Planning.

Linton, R., 1942, "Age and Sex Categories," American Sociological Review, Vol. 7, No. 5, 589-603.

Mandin, L., 2004, "Active Ageing in Europe," paper prepared for the WRAMSOC workshop in Berlin, 23-24 April. (http://www.kent.ac.uk/wramsoc/conferencesandworkshops/conferenceinformation/berlinconference/activeageingineurope.pdf).

Morioka, K., 2000, *"Koureisha no Paasonaru·nettowaaku* (Personal Networks of Older People)", Kiyoshi Morioka eds., *"Toshishakai no Ningenkankei* (Human Relationships in Urban Society)", The Society for the Promotion of the University of the Air, 162-176.

Naoi, M., 2001, *"Koufuku ni oiru tameni —Kazoku to Fukushi no Sapooto* (For Happy Ageing—Support by Family and Welfare Service)", Keisou Shobo.

Oda, T., 2003, *"Shoushikoureishakai ni okeru Saadoeiji to Akutibu·Eijingu* (The Third Age and Active Ageing in an Ageing Society with Low Fertility)", (http://www2.kobe-u.ac.jp/~oda/sympokeynote.pdf).

Parsons, T., 1942, "Age and Sex in the Social Structure of the United States," American Sociological Review, Vol. 7, No. 5, 604-616.

Taqi, A., 2002, "Older People, Work and Equal Opportunity," International Social Security Review, Vol. 55, Issue 1, 107-120.

Tsuji, I., 2004, *"Nobasou Kenkou Jumyou* (For Longer Healthy Life Expectancy)", Iwanami Shoten.

Victor, C., 2005, "The Social Context of Ageing", Routledge.

Walker, A., 2002, "A Strategy for Active Ageing," International Social Security Review, Vol. 55, Issue 1, 121-139.

Wellman, B., 1981, "Applying Network analysis to the Study of Support," Gottlieb, B. ed., "Social Network and Social Support", Sage, 171-200.

WHO, 2002, "Active ageing: A Policy Framework", (http://www.who.int/hpr/ageing/ActiveAgeingPolicyFrame.pdf).

Chapter 2

Amano, M., 1999, "Oi no Kindai (Modern Ageing)", Iwanami Shoten.

Aoi, K. and Wada, S., 1983, *"Chuukounenreisou no Shokugyou to Seikatsu — Teinentaishoku o Chuushin to shite* (Job and Life of the Middle-Aged: Centering on Mandatory Retirement)", University of Tokyo Press.

de Vroom, B. and Guillemard, A, M., 2002, "From Externalization to Intergration of Older Workers: Institutional Changes at the End of the Worklife," Goul Andersen and H. Jensen ed., Changing Labor Markets, Welfare Policies and Citizenship, Bristol: The Policy Press, 183-207.

Hiraoka, K., 1983, *"Teinentaishoku ni kansuru Taidokouzou —Fuan, Imeeji, Teinensei eno Hyouka o Chuushin ni* (Attitude Organization toward Mandatory Retirement: Fear, Image, Evaluation of Retirement System)", Kazuo Aoi and Shuichi Wada ed., *Chuukounenreisou no Shokugyou to Seikatsu —Teinentaishoku o Chuushin to shite* (Job and Life of the Middle-Aged: Centering on Mandatory Retirement), University of Tokyo Press, 147-73.

Honda (Okitsu), Y., 1998, *"Kyouikukunren to Chuukounenki no Shokugyouteki Jiritsusei* (Education and Training, and Occupational Autonomy of the Middle-Aged)", *Chuukounen no Hatarakikata to Seikatsusekkei ni kansuru Chousahoukokusho* (Survey Reports on Working Patterns and Life Planning of the Middle-Aged), Japan Institute of Labour, 28-57.

Ikeda, S., 2003, *"Shigoto·Kaisha tono Kankei* (Relationships with Work and the Company)." *Shoushikoureishakai ni okeru Sarariiman no Seikatsushuugyou sutairu no Tayouka ni kansuru Kenkyuu* (Research on the Diversity of Employees' Lifestyles and Employment Patterns in an Ageing Society with a Falling Birthrate), Research Institute for Senior Life, 21-45.

Inagami, T., 1992, *"Gendainippon no Koyoukankou —Ikutsuka no Hendoukyokumen to sono Shisa* (Employment Practice in Modern Japan: Changing Phases and Suggestions)", *Korekara no Hatarakikata Part I* (Series No. 21) (How to Work in the Future: Part I), Japan Institute of Labour, 97-126.

———, 1999, *"Souron: Nippon no Sangyoushakai to Roudou* (General Theory: Japan's Industrial Society and Labor)", *Kouza Shakaigaku 6 —Roudou* (Lecture: Sociology 6— Labor), University of Tokyo Press, 1-32, Editorial Department, Iwanami Shoten ed., 1999, *Teinengo —Mouhitotsu no Jinsei eno Annai* (Post-Retirement Stage: Invitation to Another Life), Iwanami Shoten.

Iwanami Shoten Publisher, 1999 *"Teinengo-Mouhitotsu no jinsei eno annai* (After Mandatory Retirement: Introduction to Alternative life style)".

Japan Organization for Employment of the Elderly and Persons with Disabilities, 2004, *"Koureishakai Toukei Youran* (Statistical Directory on Ageing Society)".

Japan Institute of Labour, 1998, *"Chuukounen no Hatarakikata to Seikatsusekkei ni kansuru Chousahoukokusho* (Survey Report on Working Patterns and Life Planning of the Middle-Aged)".

———, 2000, *"Deetabukku: Kokusairoudouhikaku 2001* (Data Book: International Labor

Comparison 2001)".

———, 2001, *"Shogaikoku ni okeru Koureisha no Koyou·Shuugyou no Jittai ni kansuru Kenkyuuhoukokusho* (Facto-Finding Report on Employment of the Elderly in Foreign Countries)".

Kato, J., 1988, *"Oo Teinen—150 nin no Aratana Sentaku* (Oh! Retirement: New Choices of 150 People)", Bungei Shunju.

Maeda, N., 2000, *"Shigoto to Kateiseikatsu no Chouwa—Nippon·Oranda·Amerika no Kokusaihikaku* (Harmonization between Work and Family Life: International Comparison between Japan, Netherlands and US)", Japan Institute for Labour.

———, 2002, *"Dansei no Roudoujikan to Kateiseikatsu* (Men's Working Hours and Family Life)", Kunio Ishihara ed., *Kazoku to Shokugyou—Kyougou to Chousei* (Family and Career: Competition and Adjustment), Minerva Shobo, 158-81.

———, 2003, *"Koureiki ni okeru Tayouna Hatarakikata to Anpeido·waaku eno Hyouka— Dansei Teinentaishokusha no Bunseki* (Various Working Patterns in Later Life and Evaluation of Unpaid Work: Analysis of Male Retirees)", Bulletin of National Women's Education Center, Japan, 7: 21-31.

Ministry of Labour, 1997, *"65sai Genekishakai no Seisaku Bijon—Kouchiku no tameno Sinario to Kadai* (Policy Vision of Active Ageing Society for 65-Year-Olds: Scenario for Realization and Challenges)", Active Ageing Research Committee for 65 Year Olds, Employment Security Bureau, Ministry of Labour.

Nishimura, K., 2004, *"Shoushikoureishakai to Koureihiyousha no Koyou* (Ageing Society with a Falling Birthrate and Employment of Senior Workers)", Kikan Roudouhou (Seasonal Labour Law), 206: 119-30.

Okada, S., 1976, *"Teinengo* (The Life of Retirement under the Age Limit)", Chuo Koron.

Okamura, K., 1987, *"Teinentaishokusha no Shuugyou·Fushuugyoujoutai to sono Kiteiyouin—Tokyo tonai no 60saidai zenhansou no baai* (Employment Status of Retirees and Requirements: Case Study of People in Their Early 60s Living in Tokyo)", *Shakairounenngaku* (Social Gerontology), 26: 3-17.

Okunishi, Y., 2001, *"Koureika to Koyouseidokaikaku no Houkousei—60sai Teinensei kara Posuto60sai Teinensei e* (Ageing and Directions of Employment System Reform: Retirement at the Age of 60 to Retirement in the post-60)", Atsushi Seike ed., *Shougai Genekishakai no Koyouseisaku* (Employment Policies in Lifelong Active Society), Nihon Hyoronsha, 39-84.

Policy Planning and Research Department, Minister's Secretariat, Ministry of Labour, 1995, *"Nipponnteki Koyouseido no Genjou to Tenbou* (Current Status and Perspective of Japanese Style Employment System)", Printing Bureau, Ministry of Finance.

Research Institute for Senior Life, 2002, *"Sarariiman no Seikatsu to Ikigai ni kansuru*

Chousahoukokusho (Survey Report on White-Collars' Life and Purpose in Life)".

———, 2003, *"Sarariiman no Seikatsu to Shuugyousutairu ni kansuru Chousahoukokusho* (Survey Report on White-Collars' Life and Employment Patterns)".

Rix, S., 2001, "Restructuring Work in an Ageing America," Victor W. Marshall, Walter R. Heinz, Helga Krueger, and Anil Verma ed., Restructuring Work and the Life Course, London: University of Toronto Press, 375-96.

Sato, A., 2000, *"Nippon no Roudousha no Roudouishiki* (Japanese Employees' Awareness of Work)", *Kikan Roudouhou* (Seasonal Labour Law), 194: 55-70.

Sato, H., 1999, *"Nippongata Koyousisutemu to Kigyou Komyuniti —Kokusaihikaku to sono Yukue* (Japanese-Style Employment System and Corporate Community: International Comparison and the Future)", *Kouza Shakaigaku 6 Roudou* (Lecture: Sociology 6— Labor), University of Tokyo Press, 33-73.

Seike, A., 1998, *"Shougai Genekishakai no Jouken —Hataraku Jiyuu to Intai no Jiyuu to* (Conditions of Lifelong Active Society with Lifelong Productivity: Freedom of Working and Retirement)", Chuo Koron.

———, 2001, *"Nenkin・Koyouseido ga Koureisha no Shuugyou ni oyobosu Eikyou —Shougai Genekishakai o tsukurutameni* (Influence of Pension and Employ System on Employment of the Senior: For Creation of Lifelong Active Society)", Atsushi Seike ed., *Shougai Genekishakai no Koyouseisaku* (Employment Policies for Lifelong Active Society), Nihon Hyoronsha, 1-38.

Sodei, T., 1975, *"Shakairounengaku no Riron to Teinentaishoku* (Social Gerontological Theories and Mandatory Retirement)", *Shakairounengaku* (Social Gerontology), 1:19-36.

The Japan Institute for Labour Policy and Training, 2004, *"Shuugyoukeitai no Tayouka to Shakairoudouseisaku —Kojin Gyoumuitaku to NPO Shuugyou o Chuushinn to shite* (Diversified Employment Patterns and Social Labor Policies: Noncorporate Subcontracting and Employment in NPOs)", Research Report on Labor Policies No. 12.

———, 2004, *"Kinrouishiki no yukue —Kinrouseikatsu ni kansuru Chousa* (1999, 2000, 2001) (The Future Direction of Labor Awareness: Surveys on Working Life)", Research Report on Labor Policies No. 2.

Tominaga, K. Miyamoto, M., 1998, *"Joron Nihongata Koyousisutemu no Kouzouhendou— Teichakugata Koyou kara Ryuudougata Koyou e* (Introduction: Structural Change in Japanese-Style employment System—Fixed Employment to Liquid Employment)", Kenichi Tominaga and Mitsuharu Miyamoto ed., *"Mobiriti Shakai eno Tenbou* (Perspective of A Mobility Society)", Keiogijuku University Press, 3-21.

Ujihara, S., ed., 1985, *"Toshi Koureisha no Koyoumondai* (Employment Issues for the Senior in Urban Areas)", Nihon Rodo Kyokai.

Wada, S., 1983a, *"Joron* (Introduction)", Kazuo Aoi and Shuichi Wada ed.,

"*Chuukounenreisou no Shokugyou to Seikatsu —Teinentaishoku o Chuushin to shite* (Job and Life of the Middle-Aged: Centering on Mandatory Retirement)", University of Tokyo Press, 3-18.

———, 1983b, "*Teinentaishoku no Shakaigakuteki Apuroochi* (Sociological Approach to Mandatory Retirement)" Kazuo Aoi and Shuichi Wada ed., "*Chuukounenreisou no Shokugyou to Seikatsu —Teinentaishoku o Chuushin to shite* (Job and Life of the Middle-Aged: Centering on Mandatory Retirement)", University of Tokyo Press, 52-71.

———, 1988, "*Koureisha no Shuurou* (Employment of the Senior)", *Rounenshakaikagaku* (Journal of Gerontology), 10(2): 45-63.

Walker A., 1999, "The Principles and Potential of Active Ageing: Keynote Introductory Report for the European Commission," Conference on Active Ageing, 15-16 November.

Yamaguchi, K. Kojima, H., 2002, "*Koureishahou* (Elder Law)", Yuhikaku.

Chapter 3

Japan Organization for Employment of the Elderly and Persons with Disabilities, 2004, "Statistical Directory on Ageing Society".

Japan Institute for Labour, 1998, "Survey Reports on the Working Patterns and Life Planning of Middle-Aged Citizens".

Chapter 4

Aoi, K. Wada, S., 1983, "*Chuukounenreisou no shokugyou to seikatsu—teinentaishoku o chuushin toshite* (Work and Life of Senior Age Population)", Tokyodaigaku Shuppankai

Amano S., 1999, "*Oi no Kindai* (Ageing in modern society)", Iwanami Shoten.

Atchley R., 1989, "A Continuity Theory of Normal Ageing", The Gerontologist, Vol.29, No.2, 183-190.

Depner C. and B. Ingersoll, 1982, "Employment status and social support: The experience of the mature woman" M. Szinovacz ed., "Women's Retirement: Policy Implications For Recent Research", 61-76. Beverly Hills, Sage.

Fujisaki H., 2004, "*Koureiki eno ikou to Ikigai* (Transition To Older Age And Well-Being)", Ikigai Kenkyu, No.10, 41-51.

Hatch L., 1990, "Effects of Work and family on Women's later-Life Resources", Research on Ageing, Vol.12 No.3 ,311-338.

Hatch L. and Bulcroft K., 1992, "Contact with Friends in Later Life: Disentangling the Effects of Gender and Marital Status", Journal of Marriage and the Family, 54; 222-232.

Ikeda S., 2003, "*Shigoto to kaisha to no kankei* (Work And Company For Senior Workers)", "*Shoushikoureishakai ni okeru sararii men no seikatsu to shuugyou sutairu no tayouka ni kansuru kenkyuu*", Senior Plan Kaihatsukikou (Research Institute for

Senior Life), 21-45.

Imada Y., 1991,*"Josei no caria to korekara no hatarakikata* (Careers For Women And The Future Way Of Working Life)", Nihonroudoukenkyuuzasshi, No.381, 12-24.

Inagami T., 1993, *"Koureishakoyoukanri no henka to tenbou* (Change And Prospect Of The Human Resource Management For Senior Workers)", Shimada H. and Inagami T. ed., *"Koureisha no roudou to raifudezain"*, 36-69. Daiichihouki.

Kaneko I., 1993, *"Toshikoureishakai to chiikifukushi* (Ageing Society In Urban Settings And Community Welfare)", Minerva Shobou.

Kim S. and Feldman D., 2000, "Working in Retirement: The Antecedents of Bridge Employment and It's Consequences for Quality of Life in Retirement", Academy of Management Journal, Vol. 43, No, 6, 1195-1210.

Kounenreisha Koyou Kaihatsu Kyoukai, 2003, *"Koureishakai toukeiyouran"* (Statistics Outlook Of Ageing Society).

Maeda N., 2000, *"Shigoto to kateiseikatsu no chouwa—Nihon to Oranda to America no kokusaihikaku* (Harmonization Between Work And Family: Comparative Study Of Japan, The Netherlands And U.S.)", Nihon Roudou Kenkyuukikou.

———, 2002, *"Dansei no roudoujikan to kateiseikatsu* (Working Time And Family Life For Men In Japan)", Ishihara K. ed., *"Katei to shokugyou—kyougou to chousei"*, 158-181. Minerva Shobou.

———, 2003, *"Koureiki ni okeru tayou na hatarakikata to unpaid-work eno hyouka—dansei teinen taishokusha no bunseki* (Diversifying Working Styles Of The Retired Men And Their Attitudes Towards Unpaid Work)", Kokuritsu Joseikyouiku Kaikan Kiyou, No.7, 21-31.

Masaoka H. et al., 1993, *"Teinentaishokukatei to raifusutairu—Otoko no raifucoosu* (Process Of Mandatory Retirement: Life Course For Men)", Waseda Daigaku Ningen Sougou Kenkyu Center.

Moen P., 1996, "A Life Course Perspective on Retirement. Gender and Well-Being", Journal of Occupational Psychology, Vol.1, No.2, 131-144.

———, 2003, "Midcourse:Navigating Retirement and a New Life Stage", Mortimer J. and Shanahan M. ed., *"Handbook of the Life Course"*, Kluwer Academic/Plenum Publishers.

———, Dempster-McClain D., 1989, "Social Integration and Longevity:'An Event History. Analysis of Women's Roles and Resilience", American Sociological Review, Vol. 54, 635-647.

———, Dempster-McClain and R. Williams, 1992, "Successful Ageing: A Life-Course Perspective on Women's Multiple Roles and Health", American Journal of Sociology, 1612-1638.

Naoi M., 2001, *"Koufuku ni oiru tameni—katei to fukushi no sapooto* (For Happy Ageing:

Family And Social Welfare)", Keisou Shobou.

Nishimura K., 2004, "*Shoushikoureishakai to koureihiyousha no koyou* (Aged Employees In Low Fertility And Ageing Society)", Kikanroudouhou, No.206, 119-130.

Quick H. and Moen P., 1998, "Gender, Employment, and Retirement Quality: A Life Course Approach to the Differential Experiences of Men and Women2", Journal of Ocuupational Health Psycology, Vol.3, No.1, 44-64.

Riddick C., 1982, "Life Satisfaction among Ageing Women: A Causal Model", M. Szinovacz ed., "Women's Retirement: Policy Implications From Recent Research", 61-76. Beverly Hills, Sage.

Ruhm C. J., 1994, "Bridge Employment and Job Stopping: Evidence from the Harris/Commonwealth Survey", Journal of Ageing and Social Policy, 6(4),73-99.

Sato H., 1999, "*Nihongatakoyou system to kigyou community—kokusaihikaku to sono yukue* (Japanese Employment System And Company Based Community)", "*Kouza Shakaigaku Roudou*", 33-73. Tokyodaigaku Shuppankai.

Research Institute for Senior Life (Senior plan Kaihatsukikou). 2002, "*Sararii men no seikatsu to ikigai ni kansuru chousahoukokusho* (Report For Working Life And Well-Being Of Salary Men)".

———, 2003, "*Salary men no seikatsu to shuugyou style ni kansuru chousahoukokusho* (Report For Working Life And Working Style Of Salary Men)".

Sugisawa A., Sugisawa H., Nakatani Y. and Shibata H., 1997, "*Roureiki ni okeru shokugyou kara no intai ga seishintekikenkou to shakaitekikenkou ni oyobosu eikyou* (Effect Of Retirement On Mental Health And Social Well-Being Among Elderly Japanese)", Nihonkoushuueisei Zasshi, Vol.44, No.2, 123-130.

Szinovacz M., 1982, "Introduction: Research on Women's Retirement", M. Szinovacz ed., "*Women's retirement: policy implications for recent research*", 61-76. Beverly Hills, Sage.

Chapter 5

Boissevain, J., 1974, "Networks, Manipulators and Coalitions", Basil Blackwell and Mott Ltd.

Bott E., 1957, "Family and Social Network", Tavistock Publications.

Burt P., 1984, "Network Items and the General Social Survey," Social Networks, No.6, 293-340.

Fujisaki,H., 1982, "*Roujinfuyou ni okeru kazoku・shinzoku nettowaaku to shakaifukushi saabisu no kinou bunyuu—Litowaku Sasuman no shosetsu o chuushin ni* (Functional Sharing of Elderly Care: Theories of E. Litwak and M.B. Sussman)", Jinbungappou (Journal of Social Sciences and Humanities), Vol. 157, Tokyo Metropolitan University,

57-82.

Hall A. and Wellman B., 1985, "Social Networks and Social Support," Cohen S. and Syme L. ed., "Social Support and Health", Academic Press, 22-41.

Kaneko, I., 1987, *"Toshikoureisha no nettowaaku kouzou* (Network Structure of Urban Elderly)", Shakaigaku Hyouron (Japanese Sociological Review), Vol. 38, No. 3, 336-350.

Maeda, N., 1992, *"Sosharu nettowaaku no gainen to houhou— Weak Tie gainen o chuushin ni shite* (Concept and Method of Social Networks—Theory of Weak Ties)" Jouchi Daigaku Shakaigaku ronshuu (Sociological studies), No. 16, 115-135.

Maeda, N., 1993, "Toshi ni okeru Pasonaru komyuniti no keisei-netto waku ron karano bunseki (A Study of Personal Community under Urban Conditions: Perspective from Social Network Theory)", Nihon Rodo Kenkyu Kikou Kenkyu Kiyou (The Studies of The Japan Indstitute of Labour), No.6, 35-50.

——, Meguro, Y., 1990, *"Toshikazoku no sosharu nettowaaku pataan— Shakai kaisoukan no hikaku bunseki* (Social Network Patterns of Urban Family—A Comparative Study of Social Stratum)" Kazoku Shakaigaku Kenkyuu (Japanese journal of Family Sociology), No. 2, 81-93.

Management and Coordination Agency, 1992, *"Rougo no seikatsu to kaigo ni kansuru chousa kekka no gaiyou* (Outline of a Comprehensive Survey of Post-Retirement Years and Nursing Care)", Soumu-cho Choukan Kanbou Roujintaisaku-shitsu (Statistics Bureau, Management and Coordination Agency), Japan.

Ministry of Health and Welfare, 1998, *"Heisei 9 nen kokumin seikatsu kisochousa no gaikyou* (Outline of Comprehensive Survey of Living Conditions of the People on Health and Welfare in 1997)." Kousei shou Daijin Kanbou Toukei Jouhou-bu (Statistics and Information Department, Minister's Secretariat, Ministry of Health and Welfare, Japan).

Marsden P., 1987, "Core Discussion Network of Americans," American Sociological Review, Vol. 52, No. 4, 122-131.

——, 1990, "Network Data and Mesurement," Annual Review of Sociology, Vol. 16, 435-463.

Matsumoto, Y., 1995, *"Gendaitoshi no henyou to comyunitii, nettowaaku* (Changing Urban City and Community Network)" Yasushi Matsumoto ed., *"Zoushoku suru nettowaaku* (Proliferating Networks)", Keisou Shobo, 1-90.

McCallum J., 1987, *"Teinentaishoku to kafuseikatsu eno ikou* (Retirement and Widowhood Transitions)" Shakai Rounengaku (Journal of Social Gerontology), No. 25, 61-66.

Meguro, Y., 1988, *"Kazoku to shakai teki nettowaaku* (Family Social Network)", Kanji Masaoka and Takashi Mochizuki ed., "Gendai Kazoku Ron (Contemporary Family)", Yuhikaku, 126-147.

Nobe, M., 1991, "*Commyunitii kuesuchon —Canberra ni okeru Kenshou* (The Community Question—Verification in Canberra)", Shakaigaku Hyouron (Japanese Sociological Review), Vol. 42, No. 2, 2-17.

Nojiri (Meguro), Y., 1974, "*Gendai Kazoku no Shakai teki nettowaaku—Pasu kaiseki no ouyou* (Social Network of Modern Family—Application of Path Analysis)" Shakaigaku Hyouron (Japanese Sociological Review), Vol. 25, No. 2, 37-48.

Nozawa, S., 1995, "*Paasonaru nettowaaku no naka no fuufu kankei* (Marital Relationship in Personal Network)", Yasushi Matsumoto ed., "Zoushoku suru nettowaaku (Proliferating Networks)", Keisoshobo, 175-233.

Otani, S., 1995, "*Gendaitoshi juumin no paasonaru nettowaaku* (Social Networks among Modern Urban Citizens)", Minerva Publishing Co., Ltd.

Ochiai, E., 1993, "*Kazoku no shakai nettowaaku to jinkougaku teki sedai—60 nendai to 80 nendai no hikaku kara* (Family Social Network and Demographic Generation—A Comparison between the 1960s and 1980s)", Otohiko Hasumi and Michihiro Okuda ed., "*21 Seiki Nihon no Neo Community* (Japan's Neo Community in the 21st Century)", University of Tokyo Press, 101-130.

——, 1997, "*21 Seiki kazoku e—shinban* (Family in the 21st Century -new edition)", Yuhikaku.

Prime Minister's Office, 1993, "*Koureiki no seikatsu imeeji ni kansuru seron chousa* (Public Opinion Poll on the Image of Life in Later Life)", Naikakusouridaijin Kanboukouhou-shitsu (Public Relations Office, Minister's Secretariat, Prime Minister's Office).

The International Leadership Center on Longevity and Society, 1995, "*Koureisha ga toraeru seikatsu kankyou youin ni tsuite no chousakenkyuu houkokusho* (Survey Report on the Living Environment Factors for the Elderly)".

Wellman B., 1979, "The Community Question: The Intimate Networks of East Yorkers", American Journal of Sociology, Vol. 84, No. 5, 1201-1231.

——, Carrington P. and Hall A., 1988, "Networks as Personal Communities", Wellman B. and Berkowitz S. D. ed., "Social Structures: A Network Approach", Cambridge University Press, 130-184.

Wenger G. C., 1992, "Help in Old Age-Facing up to Change: A Longitudinal Network Study", Liverpool University Press.

——, 1994, "Understanding Support Networks and Community Care: Network Assessment for Elderly People", Avebury.

Yasuda, Y., 1997, "*Nettowaaku bunseki—naniga koui o kettei surunoka* (Network Analysis - What Decides Activity)", Shinyosha.

Chapter 6

Matsumoto, Y., 1992, *"Atarashii aabanizumu riron* (New Urbanism Theory)", Hiroshi Suzuki ed., *"Gendaitoshi o Kaidoku suru* (Understanding of Modern Urban Cities)", Minerva Publishing Co., Ltd., 133-157.

Maeda, N., 1993a, "Toshi ni okeru Pasonaru komyuniti no keisei-netto waku ron karano bunseki (A Study of Personal Community under Urban Conditions: Perspective from Social Network Theory)", Nihon Rodo Kenkyu Kikou Kenkyu Kiyou (The Studies of The Japan Indstitute of Labour), No.6, 35-50.

Maeda.N., 1993b Toshikazoku no setaikan nettowaaku ni kansuru kenkyuu (Studies into Generational Networks in Urban Family, Kenkyuukiyo 5, Japan Institute of Labour,1993.

Meguro, Y., 1989, *"Kazoku to shakai nettowaaku* (Family Social Network)", Kanji Masaoka and Takashi Mochizuki ed., *"Gendai Kazoku Ron* (Contemporary Family)", Yuhikaku, 191-218

Nobe, M., 1991, *"Komyunitii kuesuchon—Canberra ni okeru kenshou* (The Community Question—Verification in Canberra)", Shakaigaku Hyouron (Japanese Sociological Review), Vol. 42, No. 2, 2-17.

Nozawa, S., 1992, *"Toshikazoku kenkyuu ni okeru aratana paasupekutibu—paasonaru nettowaaku ron karano saikentou* (New Perspective in Urban Family Studies—Approach from Personal Network Theory)", Jinbun Ronshu (Journal of Cultural Science), 42, Shizuoka Daigaku, Jinbun-gakubu (Faculty of Humanities and Social Sciences, Shizuoka University), 53-76.

Otani, S., 1993, *"Nihon ni okeru paasonaru nettowaaku kenkyuu no keifu to mondaiten* (Personal Network Studies in Japan and Challenges) (1)", Matsuyama Daigaku Ronshuu (Matsuyama University Review), Vol. 5, No. 3, 239-254.

——, 1995, *"Gendaitoshi juumin no paasonaru nettowaaku* (Social Networks among Modern Urban Citizens)", Minerva Publishing Co., Ltd.

Wellman B., 1979, "The Community Question: The Intimate Networks of East Yorkers," American Journal of Sociology, Vol. 84, No. 5, 1201-1231.

——, 1990, "The Place of Kinfolk in Personal Community Networks," Marriage and Family Review, Vol. 15, No.1, 195-228.

Chapter 7

Asakawa, T., Takahashi, Y., 1992, *"Toshikyojuu koureisha no shakai kankei no tokushitsu* (Characteristics of Social Relationships among the Elderly Living in Urban Areas)", Sougou Toshikenkyuu (Comprehensive Urban Studies), No. 45, University of Tokyo Toritsu (Tokyo Metropolitan University), 69-95.

Berkman L. F., 1995, "The Role of Social Relations in Health Promotion", Psychosomatic

Medicine, Vol. 57, No. 3, 245-254.
Berkman L. F., and Kawachi I., 2000, "Social Epidemiology", New York: Oxford University Press.
Harada, K. Sugisawa, H., Asakawa, T. Saito, T., 2005, *"Daitoshi-bu ni okeru kouki koureisha no shakai teki nettowaaku to seishin teki kenkou* (Social Network and Mental Health of the Old-Old in Urban Areas)", Shakaigaku Hyouron (Japanese Sociological Review), Vol. 55, No. 4, 434-447.
Inoue, H., 2004, *"Kaitei fukushi komyuniti ron* (Welfare Community Theory-Revised)", Kobayashi Publishing Company.
Kawachi I. Berkman L. F., 2003, "Neighborhoods and Health", New York: Oxford University Press, 2003.
——, Kennedy B. P. and Glass R., 1999, "Social Capital and Self-related Health: A Contextual Analysis", American Journal of Public Health, Vol. 89, Issue 8, 1187-1193.
Koizumi, H., Yoshimura, T. Sugiyama, K. Sugizaki, K., 2001, *"Komyuniti beisuto puranningu" ni kansuru kenkyuu rebyu* (Review on Community-Based Planning)", Toshi Keikaku (City Planning), Vol. 50, No. 5, Nihon Toshi Keikakugakkai (The City Planning Institute of Japan), 53-58.
Kondo, K., 2004, *"Shakai no ariyou to kenkou (2) —Sosharu kyappitaru* (Society and Health (2) - Social Capital)", Koushu Eisei (The Journal of Public Health Practice), Vol. 68, No. 9, Igaku-Shoin, 51-63.
Koyano, W., Ando, T., 2003, *"Shin shakai rounengaku* (New Social Gerontology)", World Planning.
——, Okamura, K., Ando, T. Hasegawa, M. Asakawa, T. Yokoyama, H. Matsuda, T., 1995, *"Toshi chuukounen no shukanteki koufukukan to shakaikankei ni kansuru youin* (Factors Relevant to Subjective Well-Being and Social Relationships of Middle-Aged People in Urban Areas)", Rounenshakaikagaku (Japanese Journal of Gerontology), Vol. 16, No. 2, 115-123.
Lawton, P., 1972, "The Dimensions of Morale", Kent D. P., Kastenbaum R. and Sherwood S. ed., "Research Planning and Action for the Elderly: The Power and Potential of Social Science", Behavioral Publications, 144-165.
——, 1975, "The Philadelphia Geriatric Center Morale Scale: A Revision", Journal of Gerontology, Vol. 30, No. 1, 85-89.
Maeda, D. Asano, J. Taniguchi, K., 1979, *"Roujin no shukanteki koufukukan no kenkyuu - moraru skeiru ni yoru sokutei no kokoromi* (Studies on Seniors' Subjective Well-Being— Measurement by Morale Scale)", Shakai Rounengaku (Social Gerontology), No. 11, 15-31.
——, Noguchi, Y. Tamano, K. Nakatani, Y. Sakata, S. Liang, J., 1989, *"Koureisha no*

shukanteki koufukukan no kouzou to youin (The Structure and Factors of Seniors' Subjective Happiness)", Shakai Rounengaku (Social Gerontology), No. 30, 3-16.

Naoi, M., 2001, *"Koufuku ni oiru tameni—Kazoku to fukushi no sapooto* (For Happy Ageing - Support by Family and Welfare Service)", Keisou Shobo.

Nobe, M., 1999, *"Chihoutoshi ni sumu kourei josei no shukanteki koufukukan* (The Sense of Well-Being of Elderly Women in a Medium-Size Japanese City)", Riron to Houhou (Sociological Theory and Methods), Vol. 14, No. 1, 105-123.

Okado, J. Hoshi, T., 2002, *"Shakai nettowaaku ga koureisha no seimeiyogo ni oyobosu eikyou* (Social Network's Effects on the Life Expectancy of Elderly People)", Kousei no Shihyou (Journal of Health and Welfare Statistics), Vol. 49, No. 10, Kousei Toukei Kyoukai (Health & Welfare Statistics Association), 19-23.

Sugisawa, H., 2002, *"Koureisha no kuoriti obu raifu kenkyuu o meguru ronten* (Issues Confronting Studies about the Quality Life of Elderly People)", Shakaiseisaku Kenkyuu (The Social Policy Studies), No. 3, 47-69.

Syme L., 2000, "Foreword," Berkman L. F. and Kawachi I. ed., "Social Epidemiology", New York: Oxford University Press, ix-xiv.

The International Leadership Center on Longevity and Society, 1995, *"Koureisha ga toraeru seikatsukankyou youin ni tsuite no chousakenkyuu houkokusho* (Survey Report on the Living Environment Factors for the Elderly)".

Wellman B., 1979, "The Community Question: The Intimate Networks of East Yorkers", American Journal of Sociology, Vol. 84, No. 5, 1201-1231.

Wenger G. C., 1996, "Support network measurement and typology development in England and Wales", Litwin H. ed., "The Social Network of Older People: A Cross-National Analysis", USA: Praeger Publishing, 117-141.

Chapter 8

Miyamoto, M., 2005, *"Choukikasuru ikouki no Jittai to Ikouseisaku* (Status of Prolonged Transition Phase and Transition Policy)", Shakaiseisaku Gakkaishi (The Journal of Social Policy and Labor Studies), No. 13, Horitsu Bunkasha, 3-16.

Miyamoto, T., 1999, *"Fukushikokka toiu Senryaku—Sweden moderu no Seijikeizaigaku* (The Strategy of Being a Welfare State—Political Economy in the Swedish Model)", Horitsu Bunkasha.

Schmid G., 2000, *"Roudou no Mirai* (The Future of Labor)", Kikan Rodoho (Quarterly Journal of Labour Law), No. 194, 17-36.

——, 2002, "Towards a theory of transitional labor markets", Schmid G. and Gazier B. ed., "The Dynamics of Full employment: Social Integration through transitional labor markets", (WZB) Edward Elgar Publishing, 151-195.

Tominaga, K. Miyamoto, M., 1998, "*Joron Nihongata Koyousisutemu no Kouzouhendou— Teichakugata Koyou kara Ryuudougata Koyou e* (Introduction: Structural Change in Japanese-Style employment System—Fixed Employment to Liquid Employment)", Kenichi Tominaga and Mitsuharu Miyamoto ed., "*Mobiriti Shakai eno Tenbou* (Perspective of A Mobility Society)", Keiogijuku University Press, 3-21.

Tanaka, Y., 2006, "*Roudou to Jikan o Saihensei suru — Doitsu ni okeru Koyouroudousoutaika no Kokoromi* (Rearranging Work and Time: The German Experiment in Redefining Employment)", Shiso (Thought), Iwanami Shoten, 100-116.

■About the author

Nobuhiko Maeda is Professor of Sociology at college of social sciences, Ritsumeikan University, Kyoto. He received his Ph.D from Sophia University in Tokyo and has been a researcher at the Japan Institute of Labour from 1991 to 2000. He has published several articles and chapters on 'work-life balance,' 'child care and work' in Japan and the Netherlands. Recently he has been engaged in the study of ageing and life course. Most recently he has published 'Sociology of active ageing: elderly, work and community' in Japanese (Minerva Press, 2006).

Address: College of Social Sciences, Ritsumeikan University, kita-ku Toji-in Kita-machi 56-1, Kyoto, 603-8577, Japan.

TRANSITION TO RETIREMENT AND ACTIVE AGEING:
Changes in Post-Retirement Lifestyles in Japan

2008年8月29日　初版第1刷発行

- ■著　　者──　前田信彦
- ■発 行 者──　佐藤　守
- ■発 行 所──　株式会社 大学教育出版
  〒700-0953　岡山市西市855-4
  電話 (086) 244-1268(代)　FAX (086) 246-0294
- ■印刷製本──　モリモト印刷(株)
- ■装　　丁──　ティーボーンデザイン事務所

Ⓒ Nobuhiko Maeda 2008, Printed in Japan
検印省略　　落丁・乱丁本はお取り替えいたします。
無断で本書の一部または全部を複写・複製することは禁じられています。

ISBN978-4-88730-863-3